THE CHRISTIAN ETHIC OF WAR

THE CHRISTIAN ETHIC OF WAR

BY

P. T. FORSYTH, M.A., D.D.

'Righteousness is applied holiness'

Wipf & Stock
PUBLISHERS
Eugene, Oregon

Wipf and Stock Publishers
199 West 8th Avenue, Suite 3
Eugene, Oregon 97401

The Christian Ethic of War
By Forsyth, P.T.
ISBN: 1-57910-220-4
Publication date 2/23/1999
Previously published by Longmans, Green, & Co., 1916

PREFACE

THIS book turns on the centrality of a real Atonement for the Christian Revelation of moral Redemption and public Regeneration. The Grace of God in Christ's Cross is not a forensic device, but the moral focus of the Universe—if all centre in the conscience, and morality is the nature of things. By a real Atonement I mean one not *shown* but *done* on the Cross, as the consummation of Christ's holy personality and its work. I do not aim here at expounding that Atonement, but at working out some of its moral implicates and results on the public and national side—a side on which a Christianity based only on Christ's teaching has been criticised as defective. An antithesis is discussed between the teaching of Jesus and the work of Christ which is none of my making. Is it necessary to say that the stress I place on the latter is not at the cost of the former, but only against the value given it by some (as others treat the Sacraments) as the thing most precious in the Grand Legacy. None ever spoke like Christ. There are no words so authoritative, so profound, so lovely. But the power, depth, and beauty of such words is ultimately due to their place in the perspective of the supreme and complete Word of Grace; which lifts them, fixes and eternalises them all in the Cross and what was *done* by the Holy there, when all saying or showing (even His) was in vain. The Kingdom of God is the great moral International. And it was set up in the Cross with the only Omnipotence—that of His Grace 'Who showeth His Almighty power most chiefly in showing mercy and pity.' His public judgments, from the Cross downwards, are gifts and blessings unto public salvation. By terrible things in righteousness are we answered by the God of our salvation. Also He is *merciful*, who giveth to every one according to his *works*—to every soul, society, and civilisation, always in mercy, entire and judicious.

At the same time I am not indisposed to find some help in a difficult situation from the notion of a standing ideal but of an *Interims-ethik* for the use of the community while it awaited the consummation of the age. That consummation, however, turned out to be the Cross; and the community became the Church that the Cross founded—with an ethic drawn (as the Apostles drew it) not from Christ's early teaching but from the more world-compelling crisis of the Saviour's 'finished work' for the Kingdom and its righteousness.

P. T. FORSYTH.

HAMPSTEAD,
June 1916.

[I have to thank my former pupil, Rev. F. W. Camford, M.A., B.D., for valuable help with proofs.]

CONTENTS

CHAPTER I

KILLING NO MURDER

PAGES

CHAPTER II

THE JUDGMENT OF CRIME BY CRIME

CHAPTER III

WAR AND LOVE

CHAPTER IV

JUDGMENT BY THE SAINTS

CHAPTER VII

CHRISTIAN LOVE AS PUBLIC RIGHTEOUSNESS

CHAPTER VIII

CHRISTIAN ETHIC LAY AND HISTORIC

CHAPTER IX

CHRISTIAN ETHIC HISTORIC AND NATIONAL

CHAPTER X

JUSTIFICATION AND JUDGMENT

CHAPTER XI

THE JUDGMENT ON THE CROSS AND IN THE FIELD

THE CHRISTIAN ETHIC OF WAR

CHAPTER I

KILLING NO MURDER

CAN a patriotism which does not stop short of killing men on due occasion be compatible with the idea of humanity and the love of mankind?

This is a question to which common sense promptly answers, No. But the reply is so obvious that it is suspicious. It was the answer given in the age of common sense and palpable logic, the non-ethical, non-historical age of the eighteenth century. The question arose with the rise of the enthusiasm of humanity amid an Illumination ruled by rationalism and sentiment. But the theoretical answer was very different from the practical. It was in France that this cosmopolitanism worked out to a practical conclusion, where it appeared with that fine tenderness to life marking the Revolution. A cosmopolitanism which dissolved nationality, and flouted historical tradition or obligation, revealed its true moral quality there, and the sentimentalism of the age followed its usual course, and ended in heartlessness. Humanity fell to be a mere abstract idea, which is morally lower than a true and free national life. 'Very few men are able to grasp the common interests of man as man. And these few have weakened their effectiveness by neglecting other and simpler bonds.' The cosmopolite idea is also much more powerless than a sound national life; for it soon passed under Napoleon into a passionate French nationalism which turned its master into its tool. The effect of this was to call out in other peoples also, and especially in Germany's war of liberation, a national reaction and revival whose effects have been very great. They have been so great there, indeed, that nationalism has swept into a fatal extreme of its own, and has discarded the idea of humanity entirely, whether as an idea or as a moral control. The egoism of the German nation has now shown itself to be no nobler than the egoism of humanity proved itself in the French Revolution, and it is equally deadly to mankind. The cosmopolite idea is vicious at either extreme. A cosmopolitan nationalism is morally as sterile as a cosmopolitan humanitarianism. The passion of world-empire by a nation is no less crushing than the régime of a denationalised humanity. The Kaiser shows the upshot of the one, as Napoleon did that of the other. And the two are one in spirit, and one in enmity to the race, its liberty and its life.

The great need of the hour is an effective international, which, of course, the Church should provide, but cannot. And amid the quarrels of nations it is not wonderful that many minds, untutored either in history or in ethic, should seek to find it in some form, like Socialism, which is indifferent to nationality and which overrides the concrete divisions of mankind by abstract ideas and artificial associations; while others, only too historic, find it in a Church unity over their heads. Of the former kind is the international of labour, or of democratic religion, and especially of cultured and churchless pietism—pervading the nations as the roots of an exotic overrun a garden; of the latter kind is the Church of Rome, also pervading the nations, but not out of relation to them—only it is an ultramontane relation, a spiritual imperialism rather than a Kingdom of God. We regard the Roman form of internationalism as not only useless to humanity (which the present attitude of the Pope to the war shows) but as mischievous to it. But no more useful is the international of an abstract spirituality, representing a humane fraternity, of which Christ is rather the type or 'pictorial image,' or, at most, the legislator, than its Creator and Bond.

The difficulties in the way of a real international are great, and they seem often insuperable, but they cannot be got over by ignoring the nations. It is more hopeful to think of federating them. The divisions of the Churches can only be dealt with by federation; they are incurable on the line of absorption in one imperial Church, or by the erasure of frontiers in an abstract and mystic fraternity. And so also the only hope of nations is by way of federation in a parity of common rights and reciprocal respect. But we must federate also with the past; for the future cannot jump into being except by violence; and then it is insecure. Humanity can be enriched only by a duly original use of history, and a development of its gifts in a creative continuity.

'Historians are seldom revolutionaries.' On the religious side an abstract and individual spirituality, which is mystic and no more, has in it the power neither of universality, nor of continuity, nor of moral wealth. It is not intelligent, for it dreads both analysis and order of thought. And it is not moral, because it is not social in its nature, it has not a Church in it. It runs but to groups. It has also the fatal fallacy of aiming at peace before righteousness, of treating love in another form than righteousness as the bond of *nations*, and of pursuing the sympathetic fraternity of man without first securing the righteous Kingdom of God. The race can be enriched only by that development of national spirit, culture, and conscience which, by a divine Kingdom, gives each people its divine and concrete place in humanity—neither over it in empire, nor outside it in quietism. The real wealth of mankind lies in a variety of free and living peoples, who will stop at nothing to assert and secure the right to exercise a common trust, right, and duty, and to live in the service of God's Kingdom. 'Without a country you are the bastards of humanity.' 'Without country you have neither name, token, voice, nor rights, no admission as brothers into the fellowship of the peoples' (Mazzini). And a great portion of this trust and duty is the care and development of the nationalities more weak or backward—such a function as England inherits in respect of the minor peoples of Europe, and has more recently assumed in respect of the peoples of India. It is an index of moral failure to care more for a religious society than for the Church, more for a trades union than for the nation.

We are to live for humanity. But humanity is real and rich, not as a chaotic sum of individuals that cohere, if at all, only in a unity so vast, remote, and feeble for them as the race, but as a federation of free nations, small enough for their members to love each other, and not large enough to lord the world. Only in the form of such a nation does the supernational unity of man come near enough to form a real nidus and a real loyalty for the individual. The first contribution on a social scale to the development of the race is not economic programmes or ideals, but national conscience and human duty—even if the room for it has to be won and held by war. Only, the war shall be under moral conditions; it shall not affront the conscience of mankind; it shall be war for righteousness, against the aggression of those nations that publicly discard moral or humane control. To discard that is to disown any national duty to the Kingdom of God and its Christian type of righteousness, and to revive the old pagan notion of a ruling race with the prerogative of power alone. And such a war shall also be without hate, with however much anger. A war for such an end is no mere tussle of rival peoples or of jealous dynasties. The express repudiation of national morality by one nation changed the whole complexion of the present war for Christian men, and raised its moral significance. It enlisted that nation in the service of the kingdom of spiritual evil under the prince of this world. And it converted the chastisement of that nation into a service of the Prince of Peace. It made it an obedience to the will of God, and a loyalty to that Kingdom of righteousness which it was the first charge of an atoning Christ to meet. He was a Christ actively atoning and not passively enduring, a Christ at once the victim and, by His active obedience, the agent of the judgment of God on earth. He so took the judgment that He exercised a greater judgment—as we hope by our obedient suffering in this war to be the agents, not wholly unworthy, of the judgment upon unrighteousness among nations. We shall see later that the religion of the situation turns on the question whether Christ's death was only an expedient of fatherly love or the act of a judgment constituent of divine fatherhood as holy. It turns on a collision of mere spirituality with a moral atonement in blood, of cultured piety with faith in public righteousness. The question whether we are morally bound as patriots to resist by arms national destruction is not *the* question for us as Christians in the present juncture (though no doubt destruction is the alternative). It takes the wider range and deeper note of the Kingdom of God. We stand for the Christian future of the world. It is whether a Christian nation is at liberty to fail among men the Kingdom of a holy God and its public righteousness of brotherly love. It was in a great act of national judgment for this Kingdom that Christ publicly died, and He committed us to the fellowship of such a death. Love and righteousness kiss each other in Him. But the form of that twofold unity between nations is not affectional love, but the moral righteousness which turns humanity to the Kingdom of God. Christian love in international form means the desire and purpose to see each man and people enjoy the free and humane life they have a right to. Twice already

England has (we believe in God's name) saved this liberty and justice for the world—once from the Armada, and once from Napoleon. She did it also in the founding of America. She is called to do it once more—to serve God's Kingdom in history, as she has the right to call each citizen to serve her. God has of late years set the world in our heart. The idea of the world possesses us now as in no former war. Humanity transcends patriotism. The very mother may say, as her son or her husband never returns, 'I have given his life, not for his country only (do not also the heathen likewise?) but for the life of the world.' For the world's life lies not in civilisation spread by the force of a 'superethical' power, but in mutual respect, consideration, contribution, and liberty.

It should be remembered that the object of war is not to kill but to bind the strong superman. And, if he is so strong, infatuate, and criminal that nothing will stop him in his unrighteousness but honest and judicial killing, such killing is not murder nor is it hate. A disabling wound would really serve the purpose as well as death, if we could inflict the one without the other, and make it last long enough for the purpose. Such war is not 'multitudinous murder.' It is a form of judgment. If it violate the right to live and be free, it does so as capital punishment does, or indeed any punishment. If killing is murder here, no Christian could be a judge, and certainly not a sheriff charged with the execution. The Jews, who had in their sacred law the precept, 'Thou shalt not kill,' killed their enemies freely in war, and stoned their citizens to death by law. The killing in war is not, like murder, a matter of personal passion, or for private ends. Nor is personal revenge for it cherished. The soldier does not act in a private capacity but in an official. He acts under trust. He is the mandatory and representative of his people. He is not his own but a member and organ of his nation. Considering what his nation has done for him in God's great grace and His long, historic providence, it has a divine claim both on his life and conscience (to say nothing of his affection)—a claim which, short of being absolute, is yet very high, and in a crisis extremely high. He is a kind of magistrate for his people. He has the benefit of Rom. xiii. 4. He administers justice in a way of duty. If a minister as a soldier shot a German, it would not affect his clerical vocation. No man can be a worse minister for having done his duty. He is not striving against individual foes, but, in the Lord's controversy, he wars against lives and consciences which have committed themselves as servants to unrighteousness. Their honour as patriots stands rooted in dishonour. And they have ceased, in their allegiance to a non-moral government, to be private individuals whose death on the field would be murder. We war in the service of the love of mankind taken as an ethos and not as a pathos, as a moral principle and not as an affection. It is quite inept to say that the loyalty of the German to his nation is as respectable as our own. That is one of the futilities that beset the moral amateur, for whom self-sacrifice has a moral value in itself whatever be the object. It has no such value, and to think it has is one of the debasements of an age whose ethic has largely fallen into an æsthetic, and become more valuable for literary and histrionic purposes than for life and duty. The moral value of sacrifice is determined entirely by the object of it. The most admiring devotion of fallen spirits to Satan in Milton's splendid Pandemonium has no moral worth but only deepens the perdition.

There are nations we must love as Jesus loved the Pharisees. War with them need not have malice in it, nor the desire to rob or destroy for destruction's sake, which is barbarism pure. The object of righteous war is not to kill, but to secure law and justice 'by a dangerous operation.' It is to enter the territory of the aggressor, and so to deal with his resources for mischief as to restore the course of things and the relations of peoples to those great supernationals, the reign of law, the control of right, and the enjoyment of freedom. Is it the Christian thing to repudiate our trusteeship of these things in the world, refuse to be fellow-workers with their God, and consent to be walked over with all our responsibilities? What are we to do when it is clear that our non-resistance to evil (even to our death) becomes the provocation of evil, offers it impunity, fosters its increase, and gives up the world to the scoundrels? How escape from the strange result of such an absolute principle, when applied to states, that only offensive wars are Christian? Christ certainly did resist evil, resisted it actively to its destruction. He resisted it, even to death in the act of doing so, and not in taking it passively. And He resisted it to the entailing of death on His many martyrs; nay, even to the infliction of death—unless we think that the destruction of Jerusalem had nothing to do with the crime of the Cross or the Judge of history. A nation which, in a race for power, disowns ethic at a national crisis (itself being judge of the occasion) cuts itself off from humanity (whose real unity and bond is in the conscience and its righteousness). And it cannot be treated except as an alien, not to say vermin, to the race, whatever goodwill may keep us ready to recognise sound repentance. Love is a relation, and its mode of action depends not on one of the parties but on both. However much we love, we cannot treat the mocker of our love as we do its respondent. The love remains constant, but the treatment does not. The father, heart-broken over his blackguard son, cannot, on an expression of penitence, take him back into the home where there are half a dozen young boys. The first charge on divine love as holy love is the practical honouring of universal righteousness. This is the profound principle lost from a religion that founds Christian ethic in the teaching of Christ and not in His death, and that cherishes love at the cost of all atonement. The end is the debasement of love.

A war like the present is not inconsistent with that grateful love of the German people which many cherish. It is a service to that people (though that is not why we do it), and its effect should be to liberate them from the hardest of taskmasters who have made the kindly German name to be a moral offence and an inhuman scandal in all the world. Public love is the desire to see all men in the enjoyment of free and righteous life. To punish the Germany that now is is to return good for evil. It is a part of the pain and conflict of the historic Redemption. By a public and negligent submissiveness that too tractable people has allowed those roughriders to get into the saddle; whose idea is not nationalism founded on law and moving in freedom to international respect, but it is empire; and it is world-empire, not simply using force but founded on force, brutal or scientific, and defying all that a humane and especially a Christian conscience calls God. It is one of their own prophets who has written—

> Next to the degree of wickedness which we call devilish is selfish and insolent imperiousness, proud and astute indifference to common moral ends, and lastly self-seeking forms of patriotism, pride of rank, and family ambition; which indeed are based on particular moral goods, but pursue them in a way which comes into collision with universal morality. All these grades of habitual sin we include in the vast complexity of sinful action when we form the idea of a kingdom of sin.[1]

Public opinion in Germany has never insisted on control, and never been allowed to get up its head and make an effectual protest for good and all, either socialist or democratic, as our English Puritanism did, even at a regicide cost. If the extravagance were allowed, it has been one of the misfortunes of Lutheranism never to have executed a king, as France and England both did to be free. And for this public crime of docility on its part the whole nation and the whole solidary world must suffer one of the most awful judgments of all history. It

[1] Ritschl, *Justification and Reconciliation*, p. 338, English edition; p. 320, 2nd German edition.

is not a task unworthy of love to deliver the German people from its political impotence before this caste, to help its old humanity and *Gemütlichkeit* to practical freedom, and to cut out its military cancer by a very costly operation. It is in soul a people worthy for whom this should be done. And the more they may scorn such service in the moment of passion, the more needful and humane it is that for the world's sake the infatuation should be cured. To extinguish in hate the great German people, even were it possible, would be no worthy object for a people of Christian culture, but it is worthy to reclaim nationality there from its crude and barbaric phase of relapse. The task may help us to work out our own salvation from such dangers. For our own freedom is not yet complete. War springs not (as Green well says) from nationality but from an incomplete nationality, a nationality that trusts to force of arms, and not to law, justice, and liberty, which are the public forms of Christian love. The best Christian thing we can give our neighbour is the Kingdom of God and its righteousness.

War is not essentially killing, and killing is here no murder. And no recusancy to bear arms can here justify itself on the plea that Christianity forbids all bloodshed or even violence. Did Christ's scourge of small cords (in the temple too) mean no more than Burke's dagger ? The individual in war is the organ of a moral State; and the State does not order him to kill but to occupy territory by a process in which the risk to life is great. And each foe takes equal risks, which in murder is not the case. But an exaggerated value put upon life in comparison with the righteousness of God is an unchristian feature in much Christianity, demoralised as it is by a long insular peace and a popular religion with more sentiment than conscience. It is a feature which would have prevented the exploration of the world, the first efforts in navigation, and most of the early stages of the subjugation of nature. We are to love our neighbour as ourself. But loving one's self does not mean sparing one's self. It does not mean cosseting our own life. The Christian man loves himself as the agent and servant in the world of God's righteous and historic Kingdom established in Christ's death. Christ died not for a scattered elect but for the conversion of history, by making the kingdoms of this world the provinces of another. The Christian man loves himself for the sake of that Christ; for Whom, and for the purposes of His death, he dies daily in whatever form duty prescribes, whether public or private. 'Godly men have a public spirit,' says Goodwin. The Christian risks his life in this interest. If he love his neighbour as himself, his Christian self, that means that it is for the same sake and for the same service. And, if he spare not his own life for the Kingdom, he must not shrink from risking his fellow-citizen's in stopping the enemy of that Kingdom when duty takes that public form. Christ ruined many careers, and brought sorrow and death to many a soul. Is there no such thing lawful to a Christian as a war of chastisement on due cause? May the nations not be the agent of God's judgment on a nation, as on a criminal? Would it be an unchristian thing for a nation to be the agent of God's judgment on the Turk for the massacres of millions of Armenians in circumstances of horror which as yet we but poorly know. And, if a nation may serve God at all in a way so solemn, is it superior Christianity for individuals in it to hang back, to live on a sacrifice of others which they contemn ?

We may be told that no Christian can take part in any action which transgresses the Golden Rule, that we should do unto others as we would that they should do unto us. I will not go into the severe change that this would bring into the lives of many who hold that view and press that rule, and who yet are remarkable successes in our radically egoist, keenly competitive war of business. But I will take the precept, and take it on the highest, and therefore the truest and most decisive, level of its application. I will take it as a great saint might take it, not according to the wishes and woulds of the average man. What form would the saint's obedience here take ? If he spoke from his saintly height, would he not say this, 'I would above all things be kept in holiness, and be kept from sin. Holiness is more than life, and sin is worse than death. I would that I might die rather than sin. And, if you are sure, by any message from God which has not reached me, that I am going in a measurable time to commit a deadly sin, I will not blame you for killing me if that be the only way to prevent it. And, if I have deserved death, I wish to give myself up to die.' The true penitent, as Luther says—*Cupit justitiam laesam ulcisci*—'I will bear the indignation of the Lord.' If such a man is to do to others as he would that others do to him, is he wrong by Christian ethic, when he perceives a deadly sin begin in his fallen brother, in treating him as he desires to be treated himself, and at least risking his brother's life in the process of averting his sin or its effects? The precepts of Christ have not a national application, as some say they have; but, if they had, and with those who say they have, it does seem as if that were not an unfair use to make of the Golden Rule in relation to the killing in war.

It is often pointed out that if there be not the right of war upon due cause on the part of a State, the refusal of taxes is entailed, not only in war-time but also in time of peace, since a huge part of the national resources is spent on an army and navy. The holder of that view is able to earn his living in comfort in a State which can keep its order and existence at a crisis only on the war principle—by police or soldiers. His livelihood is possible only on immoral conditions. To pay taxes, then, without being able to earmark them, is to be as much a partner in the war as fighting would be—with the added enormity of paying others to do an immoral thing which the protester evades by buying himself off. In so denying national brotherhood he renounces the actual, concrete, providential brotherhood, and does it through a dreamy, ideal, and self-willed one. Those who take the line I describe are art and part in the nation's war if they do not leave the country for one whose Government is pledged never to fight —whether as too good or too proud. Yet we even heal the wounded to send them back to fight again. If the purist ethic is to be thorough, its advocates could perhaps only be quite faithful by setting up a community in some vast wilderness entirely detached from history or society and their obligations. The experiment has been tried often, and it has always gone to pieces as ethical sectarianism run wild.

CHAPTER II

THE JUDGMENT OF CRIME BY CRIME

It used to be said of Lord John Russell that he was prepared at any moment to take command of the Channel fleet. And such is the self-confidence of some homespun moralists and the gay democracy. There is no national question too great, too old, or too complex to be handled on the principles which guide a home. The foreign policy of some especially would apply to the intricacy of modern problems and the relations with military or backward nations the mild methods of a mass meeting. For others, historic legacies and delicate situations make a jungle through which a straight path can just be hewn. The world would be worked on the lines of a trades-union whose *ultima ratio* is the war of classes and the battle of the strike. This is often but another phase of that unschooled passion of impatience and that faith in force which mark the idealist without experience in the actual handling of affairs. It is another phase of that faith in force which, before the war, had come to infect so many sections of society—women, workmen, or aristocrats. You must expect nothing by persuasion, only by pressure. That is the war principle. It would make law by force instead of handling force by law. It distrusts pacific methods, even with a pacifist programme. There is a curious alliance between religious pacifism and labour pacifism. Pacifism is a plank in the programme of a section of Labour which would not object in principle to a general strike if it promised success in bringing society to its knees at the cost especially of the women and children. That is a policy of force not different in kind from the Kaiser's, and it betrays the same habit of heart and mind. But it is absolutely different from all that the finer pacifism intends, which in public affairs trusts in justice even more than love. There can be no real co-operation between the two movements—between any shade of Quakerism, for instance, and the I.L.P. It is not possible, morally or economically, just to shear a path through the troubles of the time. Before urging democratic control it would give confidence if the democracy could show what controlled it.

But even to the more ethical and persuasive pacifism it may be respectfully suggested to be more subtle in order to be more true and effectual. The idealists should remember that the most inconvenient facts are largely what the ideas of the past have made them. No less than ideas they are locked in the skein of the movement of thought. They fashion the ideas of the future, even if they are not their source. They shape the form which moral action, however ideal, at any stage must take. Besides the power of glowing to ideas there is the faculty of gauging situations and weighing facts. And without a somewhat careful culture the two may be in an inverse ratio to each other; whereof the practical end is madness and *débâcle*, as Germany shows. The sense of a situation is a very different thing from the intuition of thought, and a more precious. We have a dread of casuistry which is not without ground, but, for all that, let us be alive to the intricacy of moral situations, and especially public situations, not to be seized by the thick finger and thumb that serve the individual so well in his daily job. Let us be more subtle, for it is to be more sympathetic, more understanding. Let us recognise the firstrateness of the second best. Idealism severed from historic fact, positive faith, and moral sagacity is one of the most destructive explosives known.

It seems absurd, for instance, to the very plain mind that war should be admitted to be a crime on either side, and yet recognised to be the only right course to take. But so it is, and let us repress the jibe about Jesuitry. Casuistry everyone has to practise; the question is whether we should use amateur or skilled. The short, straight, and swift road to a given point is the track of a shell, with the shell's effect. Life would be much easier if our alternatives were always a plain black or white, a sheer yes or no, a clear war or peace. We should then need but little guidance —only enough vitality to go through. But life is not so. The moment we rise beyond its most naïve and natural levels, and begin to realise what choice is in a complex civilisation, we discover that it is otherwise. Our worst difficulty is not to do the clear right; we have the other strain on us—to discern it as it rises dim from a troubled sea. And those who possess that vision are our best guides. Moral *flair* is often the most valuable kind of moral force, especially for those in any authority. We have constantly to do with junctures where our only choice is not between bald right and wrong, but between two forms of wrong—a greater and a less. In such cases an honest and experienced casuist may be of more use to us than a heroic preceptualist or an *exalté* martyr; and moral sagacity stands us in better stead than moral dictation. It is quite true, as Cardinal de Retz said, that we never come into a fix like that except as the result of some prior occasion where we did have a choice between right and wrong. But the past cannot be as if it had never been, and we have to deal with an actual situation and its moral exit. The moral exit is then a choice of evils. The only right thing to do then is not to choose the pure right but only the less wrong. And not to choose the less wrong is to choose wrongly—unless we refuse to choose at all, but stand aside and shirk the issue; which is the worst of all, and makes us accessories of unrighteousness. We then fall from being moral persons to mere animate things, and we drift along, or are swept along, on a current, without helm or oar. It may be wrong either to pay or not pay a gambling debt. The moral is, Don't gamble. But the actual duty is either the one or the other. It is un-Christian to have more wives than one. But the missionary among his converts is faced with a situation where the relevant thing is not the abstract question of monogamy but the concrete one, whether the convert with half a dozen wives is to send five adrift with their families, or to go on with his existing obligations without adding more. It is a matter of choosing the minor wrong. To take the stale case. If a bully meet you with your wife in a lonely road, it may be a choice between sacrificing his life or the honour of one to whom you are under the marriage oath of protection. To say you must not kill him, if he so insist that there is only killing for it, to say life is so sacred that even his may not be taken at need in such a case, but you must stand by and trust God to strike the man helpless before his crime—to say that is simply to discard morals and trust miracles. It is throwing on God the dirty work you were called to do. It is to step out of the category of moral beings. It is to tempt God and force His hand. We could not continue to make much of human life unless we loved honour more than that.

The only course left at a given juncture may be the violent solution of war. It is pedantic at such a time to talk about two blacks not making a white. Brown may be practically better than either, and the only possibility. It is pedantic also to talk of war being no solution. Of course it is no rational solution. And, were mankind chiefly rational, the remark would have its effect. But mankind is not. And it would not be entirely admirable if it were. The solution of life and the world is not chiefly rational. If war is to be abolished it must be by other than rational means. It must be by means which change the man much more than his conclusions or even convictions. It is beside the mark also to say that war settles nothing except who is best equipped and endowed for it. That is not the case. It settles the past at least. It is the end of an age. This war definitely ends the Victorian age. The issue behind all war may be much vaster than the clash of rival nations, and in this case it certainly is. What we might think the juster of the two sides might lose, but the conflict is not therefore futile for the large course either of the world or of the Kingdom of God. Evidently God has another purpose with history than just to reward the good and punish the bad in a distributive way. He is working out a purpose of Redemption whose goal in a Kingdom is sure to our faith but His method is hidden to our sight. It is more didactic than useful also to tell us that war is the renunciation of Christian ethic. Of course it is. But that would be a good consideration to offer only if mankind were Christian. It would then be to the point to tell them that they were renouncing their own moral principles. As a matter of fact men are mostly not Christian. Their ethic is not Christian even when their creed is. And to offer the esoteric Christian ethic for public use when national passion is rising or loose is to stroke a crocodile or tickle a tiger. The right and fit thing to do then is to fall back on an inferior ethic and make the best of it. Christ was not among the ineffectual doctrinaires. His Sermon on the Mount had not the nations of the earth in view, deeply national as His work and crisis were. It contemplated the social ethic of individuals, and of regenerate individuals. In so far as it thought of relations with the world, it was the relations of Christian individuals to pagans, not of State to State. Also it concerned Christian relations not to sympathetic pagans, but to pagans who persecuted the Christian ; and who persecuted him because of his Christianity, and not because he was a disagreeable Christian. Until men become Christian indeed, junctures will arise in which, when everything has been done, nothing is left for it but war—unless we are prepared to give everything up to the devil, and see the world overrun by his angels; unless, that is, there is no alternative for a conscience between the highest Christian ethic and moral anarchy. If the Christian man live in society, it is quite impossible for him to live upon the *precepts* of the Sermon on the Mount. But also it is not possible at a half-developed stage to live in actual relations of life and duty on its *principle* except as an *ideal.* (We shall see later what the practical principle is in contact with a semi-pagan society.) Those who have been very urgent about Christ's precepts have yet, in many cases, made great fortunes by a skilful and earnest use of the commercial and competitive conditions on which society works, and which represent the peaceful form of the war principle. That form may be thrown off at any moment. German commercialism has revealed its true nature and ambition in its militarism at the select hour. But even the peace form does not set forth the principle of the Sermon, and the successful Quaker must bow in the House of Rimmon, and enjoy all the securities of a society on the natural level, protected in the egoism of business by police and soldiers. He must do so even in the pushing of his principles. He uses the facilities and practices of an alien and unchristian social order to do so. He is not to be blamed. He is honestly trying to convert business. Only as he uses business in a way to transcend its egoist principles so let him consent to use war.

So let him not think that he is profiting nothing by the worldly and the war idea, and lending no countenance to it. He is. He profits much.

Of course war is far below the Christian level. Society altogether is, and will long be. The fallacy is to suppose that it is a Christian ethic or none with us, that the only Christian ethic is preceptual, that a man can live anywhere but in a prairie or a balloon on a purist and unhistoric interpretation of the Christian ideal. That ideal is not a matter of precept but of principle. And principle can only work through personalities, which cannot be thoroughly moralised till they are born again. Principle which is to affect society works by permeation and not by insulation, by inspiration and not injunction.

We have another example of the literal, purist, and doctrinaire fallacy offered in connection with the ideal of Christian perfection and sinlessness. The perfect thing is really perfect growth. It is doing the very best for Christ with the actual situation, and preparing a better, with which again the same must be done. It is not retiring from it. It is making the most of it for the final consummation. It is leavening time with Eternity. 'As many of you as are perfect do so and so.' Yet, in the next breath, 'Not as though we were already perfect, but we press on.' The state of sinlessness has been regarded by many pietists as the total, not to say sudden, extinction of sin from a certain point of life onward. But such is not the New Testament view. There it is enough, for earthly life at least, that sin should not have dominion. It may recur, but always with diminishing frequency. The other principle is all the time gaining ground. Battles are lost, but the campaign is being won. The converted drunkard may relapse more than once without losing faith or hope. The falls grow fewer and fewer. If otherwise conceived, sinlessness is abstract, and may become puerile. It is a question of our real lord before it becomes a question of our actual habit, of what commands us and not of our degree of success with the new obedience. Christ is our perfection, not we ourselves, so long as His dominion grows in us and over us.

The fact is that there is a whole moral tract of progress between egoist anarchy and Christian ethic over which the world is making its painful and dreadful way; that this tract of moral growth is not without God or the action of His righteousness; that God, with Christ in final view, God in Christ, has His ways of dealing actively with evil on that plane, and requires our help and service there; that we may so stand aloof in an idealist excellence that our faith fails Him in His hour of need and agony. We may desert our Lord while we follow a dream of good in which we slip out of the providential order where He has set us and our task. We have to do our Christian part in a moral region which is below the level of Christian ethic but not of Christian duty, and which is not detached from our righteousness, nor unhallowed by conscience. The natural conscience can never replace the supernatural, but it can never be detached from it. It is its fore-court, its prelude, its minority, its schoolmaster. The stage of moral growth which is below the Christian ethic is still within the world-righteousness, the world-rule, and the historic movement of the Christian God, and it has its divine lien upon the conscience of the Christian man even when the Christian height cannot be attained. The economy of the God of Redemption is still latent in the Judaist and legalist stage of every people; and the righteousness of that stage is still in the scheme and movement of the Kingdom of God, however inchoate. Our final Christian Redemption is to our present Christianity what that was to Judaism, but our present stage is not therefore unchristian. In adjusting our moral methods from our height to the crudity of those below, in doing to the least of these, Christ's brethren, the kind of righteousness that fits and raises their moral stage (as when we teach children to do the right thing by bribes or prizes, or when we take a business case to law) we do it unto Him. This is not mere naturalism, for we do not rest there. We do not canonise that stage, we only tolerate it and improve it out of existence. There are concessions for hardness of heart, like the State law of divorce. An eye for an eye and a tooth for a tooth is not now Christian, but it was the Christianity of its time. It was a great advance and curb in its time on the mad and indiscriminate revenge where penalty had no proportion to crime, where Lamech boasted of killing a young man for merely hurting him. And in such a stage it had its divine right and obligation. The elements of this world are not all undivine. And if we can replace them by no higher principle at any juncture it is wrong to deny their right. Without them the better cannot come, but the worse may come easily enough. The consecrated life (in the pietist sense of the word) is not always the moral life. It is often but individualist, sometimes egoist, and occasionally unpleasant. And it is on the wrong moral track when it sees no divine value or duty in any conduct except what is inspired by a frame of feeling distinctly Christian. Action without Christian ideas may yet be in the Christian interest and service. The unconverted man who makes righteousness the first thing is higher than the converted who makes it but second or third by a false notion of charity. The unregenerate are not morally worthless, however helpless, before Christ's God.

A Christian nation like our own, that was growing rapidly more Christian in its social sympathy and action, may yet have, in a fight for its life, to defer some of these ideals, and turn aside, and go down from the new transfiguration into the valley to deal in Christ's name with the lunatics there, lest all divine righteousness be lost for the world. What is quite intolerable is that a Christian nation should sacrifice everything for generations to its army, and spend its supreme force in cultivating a militarist policy for the conquest of the world, and in preparing deliberately, and with the support of its Church, a situation in which a Christian ethic can have no place or possibility. That is casting off the Kingdom of God with ostentation. To make such a policy impossible is a Christian duty, even if it mean some considerable postponement of the Christian ideal, and a temporary reversion to that stage of ethic which God did employ, but which He was labouring to leave behind. The old is better for the moment, and for the purpose forced upon us by contact with peoples as yet in the stage we had hoped *we* were leaving behind. It is not always reactionary to go back or go slow. The brake is a real instrument of progress. Unless we are to deny all providential care by God of inferior civilisations, He Himself goes back from the final ethic of His Son to grasp and guide up to it the more natural and barbaric stage. God Himself, who has all the stages of discipline in His service, has to go back on occasion to one mainly outgrown. Every time He uses disease to punish sin or calamity as the end of crime He goes back to the use of force. He has His divine opportunisms and compromises, which are so far from being surrenders that they are disciplines. They are not concessions for peace but strategies for a purpose, not arrangements for safety but policies of salvation. The better day is dawning on the whole. We can mark its growth. We can sometimes trace the way in which He is forwarding the better stage by action relevant to the inferior conditions. He does not do evil that good may come; but, evil being there, He uses it to its own destruction, and He uses us in such action. He directs the minor crime so as to be a judgment on the greater. A Christian might make his public protest against war, and then go and take his part in the Lord's controversy on the battlefield as a second best. A Christian might work with all his might against the outbreak of a revolution, but, failing there, he might take his place on one or other side of the civil war. He might even obey the new government as an accomplished fact, of which he had to make the Christian best, and turn it to the most account for the Kingdom of God, which uses many forms of government, and even exploits war, though it must not provoke it or cultivate it as a policy. Man's eruptions are always being used as God's corrections, and his wrath can work the righteousness of God. The crime, or the crimes, of a French Revolution may be the only means of abolishing the prior and Satanic situation.

Often it has been pointed out how sin is punished with sin. The penalty of sin is more sin, and more complicated sin, as murder needs not only more murder, but also lying, and always cleverer lying, to cover it up. But does this mean the consolidation of the realm of sin, and the gradual matting up of the world in its tissue? It cannot mean that. For, while the growth of good consolidates good, the growth of sin is really solvent in its effect. The more sin, the more distrust and the less solidarity. It dissolves the personality, and it dissolves the society; while goodness unites both the heart and the people. So God, moving in His mysterious way, and mocking by His ironic subtlety both the clever devilry of the wicked and the merely stalwart ethic of pedantic impossibles, sets sin against sin, plays one sin off against another, and by one brings another to naught. God's will is done when sin with the sin uppermost is destroyed by sin with the sin in hand. He accepts war to destroy war. If in any juncture the exit is but by the minor wrong, it is less sin to use the minor evil than it would be to stand aside, however devoutly, and let God's enemy have free course and be glorified. And there are such junctures for all but quietists, who can be used by the devil with more effect than they let themselves be used by God. God is not the less holy because in His government of the world He employs sin against sin, and sides with the minor ill to bring the mightier to nought. He accepts a situation He did not create; but He accepts in a very concrete way—to create the new situation out of it. In a concrete, historic way, I say. The crude notion is that God should by His holy and uncompromising power override and bear down human sin, dropping fire from heaven on it, but not working through it in a strategy. That is an outcrop of the immoral passion for miracle in morals. 'I will not attack the bully who attacks my wife. If God wills that she shall escape He will smite him to the ground.' That is tempting the Lord our God. It is putting life before honour. God does not act so. He uses men. He comes to judgment with His saints. It is by a way of history that God deals with human evil. He did so conclusively in the historic Cross of His Son; who was not crucified in the sky as a spectacle, but as the result of a very concrete national situation, which He did not shirk and did much to create. He might conceivably have shirked it, and wandered humbly and piously about the world, giving the public no offence, holding conferences of the mystic-minded, and 'deepening the spiritual life.' But He forced a national issue, and brought it to a head which shortly meant the devastation of Judea, the destruction of Jerusalem, volumes of misery, and torrents of blood. He knew it involved this. He meant that judgment on Israel. And, if all this be dismissed as Jesuitic subtlety and casuistry, it can only be by discharging God from the strategy of history, or reducing His Providence to be a mere spectator of the game of peoples, with an occasional blow when it broke bounds. But His way of reconciliation comes closer to things than that. He takes a hand in the game. His method reflects the combination of wrath and mercy, of Judgment and Grace. These are one, for they are both harmonious in Himself, and they are directed on the same object with the world. I should go a long way to hear a discourse by a competent person with the views I am rejecting if he would let me suggest his text. It would be Romans xi. 28. 'As touching the Gospel they are enemies for your sake; but, as touching the election they are beloved for the Father's sake.' God both hates and loves the same object, slays him and makes him alive, makes war, and through it judgment, and thereby peace. In the present situation such a principle means among other things that we may hate the German State of to-day in the name of the same God as teaches us to love the German people for the sake of a past generation of culture and world-service, and for a present remnant of those who would rather continue that note than sink to the 'high politics' of the hour, only they are overborne. This seems a silly subtlety to a certain blunt or slashing type of mind—that God should hate and love the same object. But then St. Paul was such a Jesuit. He actually thought that men as they are were hateful to God, Who loved them for what they might be if He had His way with them as He took it in Christ. They incur the hostility of God and His judgment as they defy His Gospel and Kingdom, yet He loves them into the service of both by His very judgments. We love Germany as Christ did the Pharisees to whom He gave no quarter. And it were better that very many of these our brethren should be killed, and their nation paralysed (as with old Israel) than that their policy should destroy the world's righteousness and the humanity of the Kingdom of God among men. For if Germany won it is the moral order of the universe that would be confounded. Christ loved Israel to its destruction for the sake of that Kingdom of God which He loved more, and for which He counted His life not dear and His blood well shed—more precious blood than man's. One of the boons of the war may be to lift the pietist type of faith to a more cosmic and moral note.

War is the greatest of all the awful and complex moral situations of the world—second only to the final judgment day. It is a moral monstrosity if only because it is purely destructive. It is moral pestilence. It is a wrong on both sides. But it may be the only moral choice left. It may be the less of two immoralities, and, in so far at least, a negative contribution to righteousness. It is the course more promising morally at the particular juncture. For peace at any price can be the abnegation of morality entirely, the refusal of even a negative contribution to righteousness. After all we have done to set India on its feet and keep it in trust till its population is of political age, it would be a greater crime than war to leave it as a promenade for such a Germany as has now been revealed. At the present time it was a choice for us between war and allowing the world to be overrun by a power whose avowed programme is to sacrifice everything to power, and to abjure national morality whenever it thought that its own interests demanded it. This policy is to attack humanity, to declare war on righteousness, and to kill the very Kingdom of God in the eye. And to arrest it is the duty of those who believe in that Kingdom if it is still conceived as a Kingdom of world-righteousness in a moral Redeemer unto blood, and not merely as a sect of the gentle way in a blessed saint. Christ's world salvation hung on an act of saving judgment, and judgment is still a factor of the saving sum. And if you say man may not be the agent of God's judgment you simply rule Providence out of the interior of history.

What religion most needs is moralising especially on the social scale. But it has become demoralised by a sentiment which kills moral sympathy when, in the name of superior religion, people can stand by in a pious paralysis, and see a whole nation and its Church confessing in public and responsible words the moral repudiation I have named, exalting cruelty to be a line of policy, and pursuing an education which gives its children a holiday to rejoice and play because of the 'Lusitania.' And can it be said that it is a moralised religion that encourages men to sit at home making money and feeling good within a ring of safety and comfort made by the corpses of our best—to sit at home inditing peace, and write off their sacrifice as an inferior morality? If that be

Christ, conscience has outgrown Him. It may or may not be the priggery some call it, but it is losing Christ's eternal Cross in His occasional precepts. It is severing the sacrificial instinct of love from its moral tonic and saving element of holy judgment, even to blood. It is only a proletarian ethic, which loses moral passion in ready sentiment, is indifferent to moral appeal if only there is tangible kindness, and welcomes the almoner with his doles while it stones the prophet with his call. There is now, indeed, no chosen nation as nation, no nation with a divine reversion of the world. God does not thus prefer one people to another. But still a nation is elect to service and sacrifice for the righteousness of the divine Kingdom. It owes to that service its real and final right to exist. And the present issue has long ceased to be—ever since Belgium it has ceased to be—a struggle between peoples equally egoist and ambitious, to whom the Christian moralist could say, 'A plague on both your houses.' It has become a contest for the righteousness of the New Humanity in the Kingdom of God now by one side openly disavowed. We are free to believe that this is the act of the German State rather than of the German people. But till the nobler people deal with this ignoble State, and free themselves from it, they must share the responsibility.

In the German view a nation at a crisis must be absolutely egoistic. It has no morality. It founds the State on force. It disowns humanity. It rejects the idea of a Kingdom of God. It feels entitled to sacrifice the whole of humanity to its own safety and monopoly. It is a member of no greater society. There is no power above the State.

In a word it is not a moral entity. This is not even Hebraic. It is purely pagan. It is worse. It is Satanic. It fears no God and regards no man.

This is a monstrosity greater to moral insight than the war it causes. If an individual spoke like that we should call him devilish, and rally our Christian effort to destroy the works of such a Satan and save the public from him. The enormity is even greater when a body like a nation does it, which can only cohere in the principle of membership and sacrifice. We all unite to reject such a worse than pagan view. A nation is a moral entity in the grand style. It has creative traditions and corporate duties. It has moral entails transmitted through ages, moral judgments pursuing it through centuries, and moral glories fertile for centuries yet to be. It has world duties as surely as souls have, though their form may not be the same. A soul is saved by the righteousness of faith which may lead to the suffering gladly of wrong, but a nation is saved by the righteousness of the Kingdom's works and the public judgments of God. It has outward duties prescribed by its place in the fellowship of nations as truly as those of individuals are prescribed outwardly by their place in the living society in which they are held. They are positive, national responsibilities to God's Kingdom in the world, according to the quasi-personality that belongs to the nation as a moral unit no less necessary or sacred for humanity than the family. Righteousness is the public form of love.

And yet pacifism disowns one of the first of these duties; which is not to make war, but to see that public righteousness is done, even at the cost of war with the nation that lives for making war, and whose whole organisation is entirely subordinate to that end. To renounce that responsibility is to disown a national morality when a great crisis of public righteousness comes. It is to accept the German ethic. It is to say that the nation in a world crisis has no ethic, no positive duty as a nation to God's Kingdom, that individuals may take up certain forms of philanthropy and religious culture, but they may not abet a positive ethic in the nation, or a duty to its past and its place—only the negative ethic of keeping out of things (and coining money). It repudiates in practice the principle of active, concrete, national duty both to our people and to the world, and especially to the weak peoples. The nation, in a struggle for existence to serve universal justice, liberty, and chivalry against an immoral power which expressly repudiates all three, has no moral call, and has no right to require the help of its members to do its public duty to God's Kingdom on earth. Extremes meet. That is in principle the German position—no national obligation to God's Kingdom on earth. The one puts peace before righteousness as the other puts war. But the principle is the same—abstract and non-political piety (in which Germany abounds) at the cost of historic and public righteousness—sentimental religion of a pietist cast, which must not meddle with drastic politics —only, 'business as usual.' Yet a world righteousness is the one purpose of Him Who in His Cross has a property in every soul, and a lien on every conscience. The mightiest of the world forces is the historic purpose of a righteous God.

CHAPTER III

WAR AND LOVE

There came into my hands recently the prospectus of a society for the promotion of a pacifist programme on religious lines. It may be useful to take this programme as one disquieting symptom of a tendency in recent religion which takes many other forms, all indicating the impotence of a type of religion which preaches love without judgment either in the Cross, or history, or life, a love which seems wholly sympathetic, and if righteous at all only on the individual scale which takes saintliness for salvation.

The document runs as follows :—

> 1. That Love, as revealed and interpreted in the life and death of Christ, involves more than we have yet seen, that it is the only power by which evil can be overcome, and the only sufficient basis of human society.

One seems to have heard this note before, with its winsome ideal and its moral inadequacy. Certainly Christian Love involves more than we have yet seen. There is nothing so luminous to whose deep nature we are so dull. But are our friends going to deepen our vision ? I wish they could. But it can only be done by a Cross they do not seem to grasp, whose first loving concern with an evil world is, for both John and Paul, righteousness at any price

(Rom. i. 17). Love has its place rather within the Church than between societies like nation and nation, where it reigns as righteousness. There is no suggestion that the Love canonised in this programme is more than sympathy at Christian pitch, or that Christian truth is more than the inner light turned full on. There is no suggestion that the New Testament has to deal with something a world more than love as the instinctive heart understands it, namely *holy* love, love as the moral absolute, with a heart of grace and a method of judgment; that the prime note of the Cross of Christ and of the love there is the note of God's righteousness in a universal and eternal Kingdom, a righteousness that did not spare His only Son; that this righteousness was by that Cross much more than revealed and interpreted; that it took action there once for all as the crisis in the one historic conflict of the whole moral universe; and there set up the principle that makes the kingdoms of the world, by a holy war, but provinces of the Kingdom of God. There is no sign of a suspicion that the chief source of recent religious degeneration is the abuse of love by its severance from this righteousness; or that the great International we weary for is something much more virile, searching, and effective than Love as here put. There is no wisdom offered for our guidance in that hardest of questions—how to adjust an abstract ideal to the duties of our relative and actual situation. Any amateur can put up a *non possumus*. The project betrays a somewhat cloistered idea of life and the world in its sanguine conviction that Love, reinforced by Christ, is going to end evil and establish society. But the one thing needful is neither to love nor to perceive the excellency of love, but it is the certainty that at the long last this blessed power is going to win. The Christian gift to us is not Love but Love's final and eternal mastery. And we can be sure of that (i.e. love is worth while for life, and is a foundation for religion) only if in principle it *has* won. And that is secured in the Act of Christ's Cross for ever. But it is so secured only through the final conquest of evil there, its last judgment by the holy, and the practical hallowing there of the righteousness eternal. It is secured by something there which is not even remotely suggested by the type of religion and reconciliation represented by the programme under notice. What that offers us is but the religious counterpart of the literary sect of a generation ago whose motto was 'Love is enough.'

And, generally, the religious basis of this sympathetic but too facile idealism misses what has been called the moral cruciality of the Cross for the world—the utter perdition from sin in society, and the final tragedy of salvation by its judgment. A covering statement says that our only hope is a change of heart. 'And this is the change of heart—to renounce selfishness and to live in love.' It is the note of the mystic group with a faith non-positive and churchless, a saving faith in spiritual works. It is the climax of a generation of genial and gentle religion with the nerve of the Cross cut; which, therefore, breaks in our hand at a great historic crisis for lack of the moral note, tonic, radical, and redemptive. A loving heart and selfless life not only cannot save a world that beards the holy but it cannot come by volition. It could not come even by our being shown what Love is in an exemplary or inspiring Christ. And do we think of Christ as unselfish? It is like calling Mürren pretty.

'There is but one thing—that men shall live by the law of love. What love is we know from the life, the teaching, the death of Jesus Christ. [Is the death of Christ but a source of knowledge?] He bade us love God and our neighbour as ourselves; [and He might have bidden us till doomsday, even with the emphasis of death, and to little purpose, if He did no more than turn on this inner light]. In His life He showed us His love in practice; [And nothing but this love? Toward the Pharisees, for instance ("You vipers"), or Herod ("You fox")?], and in the hour of death He faced evil with love—entering the conflict with no other arm, showing [still but expository preaching on His part—not overcoming the world for us but showing us how to do it] the world once for all that the one sure way of overcoming evil is not to oppose it with violence but to confront it with an unfailing love [still but showing it, as if a wounded saint should make the soldiers fall back by holding up the crucifix with a heavenly smile. Nothing about the creation there of a redeemed world].'

Was there no awful judgment in that death? Did it not doom evil once for all, and, in Christ's own view, destroy the vast and regnant personality of Satan? Did it not mean, did Jesus not know it meant, the destruction of Jerusalem and of Israel in blood, the ruin of city and nation in war? Did the God reconciling in Christ not inflict that doom? Is war never His judgment, never His instrument? Could the damnability of sin as man's most anti-godly *act* be met by the mere exhibition or even exercise of a pity or *affection*, which, in its inadequacy to the moral situation, can only be called sympathetic? There is no recognition in this religious type of the saving love as *holy* love—saving and eternal only as holy. The entire idea of a righteousness holy in God is absent from such a conception of Christ—the whole idea of moral action, crucially and finally holy, as the crown of Christ's personality, the idea of divine judgment as the historic agent of salvation. Of Christian faith as the New Testament means it, as psychologically the creator of Christian love and the justification of Christian life, as its ethical principle and moral standard, there is no word; nor of the conscience and its redemption; nor of God's judging grace at all as the world's hope. It is not a creed that is missing here, nor even a theology, but a power—the principle that makes Christianity an ethical religion by the holy nature of its creative Act. The creative source of Christian ethic as of Christian life is the Cross of Christ; it is not the Sermon on the Mount, which is largely directions for certain situations, or guiding illustrations of the action of the Christian righteousness in given circumstances; at any rate it must be interpreted by the Cross. But what we have in the document I discuss is a salvation by spiritual work, by moral or religious accomplishment, as if we were saved by virtue of our faith instead of by its means. And the effort is on an individual and philanthropic scale, not on a world scale, an evangelical scale, the scale of the conscience. It is unequal to world-crises. It is the note of a remote, inexperienced, and cloistered Catholicism, carrying in it not a superior ethic but a decadence of the Gospel, a salvation of the world by charity, not by faith. On another side the plea is the recrudescence of the old Quaker dislike for the idea of a real atonement and the judgment therein. It is a defect in Barclay's fine apology. (How striking, and at bottom very instructive, is this elusion by such a people of the conscience of the supreme crisis of the conscience in the world!) There is no suspicion shown that the reconciling of the world was more than kind service to man, more than a making it up between God and man at Christ's plea to us, more than the clearing up of our distrust and an affectional rehabilitation; there is no sign that it involved the whole issue of cosmic righteousness. There is no notice of the fact that, just to protect the idea of reconciliation (2 Cor. v. 20) from this merely sympathetic view of it, and to give it its fundamental moral note, Paul follows the word of reconciliation at once with the intrinsic ground and ethic of it (ver. 21) as founded on an offering first made to God and His judgment, and resting on a righteousness made ours by Christ's being made sin for us, and not a mere suffering Lover. Whatever that abysmal phrase means it means much more than the lovely eyes of kindly love can see in reconciliation and its world fellowship. Where that communion is taken quite seriously, as in a Church, it is held that the God of holy love has power to make even hate serve reconciliation in righteousness. He can make it not only change into love, but, while acting as hate, yet be working out the purpose of love by the greatest irony in the Universe. He can force His royal judgment into the realm of evil, harness Satan himself, and divide his empire in civil war. In so acting He does not do evil that good may come, but He sets one existing evil against another, using man's lesser crime to destroy his greater, wielding evil against evil, waging just war to defeat unjust,[1] and by sin judging sin unto salvation. Reconciliation can only come by righteousness even in blood, by a tragedy of righteousness in the Cross more awful than war; it does not come by mere conciliation; and God, Who can make man's wrath His praise, Himself takes the tragedy and makes the righteousness. By His holy wisdom and moral majesty He used the crime of Israel on Christ to destroy crime, and to be, in the region where the goal is already won and where a thousand years are but as one day, the violence that ends violence, and the war that ends war. But the reconciliation this programme means is not the Christian Reconciliation. And this war is not a tussle of Chauvinist patriotisms but an issue of the world-righteousness at strife with a nation that publicly and expressly treats morality as non-existent for a nation at its choice. That is war declared on the Kingdom of God.

The programme proceeds—

2. That in order to establish a world order based on love, it is incumbent on those who believe in this principle to accept it fully, both for themselves and in their relation to others, and to take the risks involved in doing so in a world which does not yet accept it.

3. Therefore as Christians we are forbidden to wage war . . . and are called instead to a life service for the enthronement of Love in personal, social, commercial, and national life. [Called to let the war-makers capture the world for their ethic meanwhile ?]

[1] See T. H. Green's *Principles of Political Obligation*, Works, II. 466.

It is all very amiable, and ideal, and inert—all like the pictures of a seraphic Saint John, when the beloved disciple should have a face graved and lined with the furrows of the wrath of the Lamb. There is no conception here of the Cross of Love as the great Day of Judgment. There is no allusion to the Christian faith of the Kingdom of Love as already won for good and all, and already established in Christ's final overcoming of the world in His blood. All is to be due to our effort (inspired or consecrated, but tentative, and therefore problematic, always) to establish a reign of Love, to serve man in a spirit of Love ideal but not positive. It is not due to our witness by action to God's act of gracious war, which did not shrink from blood to put His holy Love, in a righteous Kingdom, beyond all that is tentative into the region of accomplished things.

The movers in this enterprise are clearly people whom it must be pleasant to have anything to do with, but are they not offering sugar-coated pills for an earthquake? Are they not stroking the crocodile? Such a religion cannot make its way in the world. That is, it cannot bring God's Kingdom in. It is too soft to keep a cutting edge, and it is not soft enough to meet the passion of men for a soft religion. Far from reading the meaning of events, the authors do not seem to know the meaning of words. The covering address says—

> He who accepts this way of life [by the bye, Christianity is not in the first instance a way of life] cannot, even for what may seem a noble and worthy end, injure the bodies and souls of other men.

What does injure mean? Inflict injustice or

inflict pain? If the former, it begs the question (as if all infliction were injury), or it utters a truism. We all agree (except the German Chancellor) that we must not treat people unjustly in soul or body. On the other hand, if it mean that no man's skin may be hurt or pained for a worthy object, it is absurd; and it would have deprived many of the discipline which was such a means of grace to their earliest years. Of course, it unlocks all the jails, and takes out of Christ's hand the whip of small cords. It is Tolstoyism. It is a useful protest but a useless policy.

Christian love is not first the form of love which Christ prescribed to those already His own in certain situations, but the love in God which Christ's whole life and death exert and reveal. That love in God so dealt with the whole moral situation of the race, its holy righteousness so dealt with a grand world-unrighteousness, as to inflict the violence of the Cross, sparing not even His Son. That is the Gospel light in which to read the Gospels. God so loved, on such a principle, so unsparingly, as to do that Son's body and soul the 'injury' of the Cross. That is the principle on which God's love dealt with the vast evil of the world. He reserved for Himself what He forbade Abraham to do. He took His Son's willing life. That is the principle of God's redeeming action in history. And it keeps war still within His providence.

The address goes on—

> But—and this is the point—he must accept this obedience [to the supposed example and law of Christ] *absolutely*. [Italics not mine.] He will be unable to consent or to participate in methods, and customs, and industry which exploit his fellow-men.

Has the writer any idea of what language means here—absolute refusal to profit by the methods of either war or commerce, of exploitation or competition in any way. We could understand a protest, and a submission under protest, to the egoist or the capitalist stage of society, a bowing in the House of Rimmon, a compliance so far as enabled the protester to convert commerce from within, and to work at the education of society for a stage higher still. But *absolute* refusal to benefit thereby means action far more serious than the founding of a new league—a step which is an infliction on the public rather than on its promoters. It means entire separation from current civilisation. It means a monastery in a prairie. It means a refusal of the comfort and safety provided for the denouncer of war by the immoral and loveless work of the trenches. It means abstinence from the food which is brought to his door by the aid of a navy which protects these methods of competition and exploitation. It means that any of this society who, at the Universities and elsewhere, live upon scholarships, or any form of charitable foundation and bequest, should renounce them forthwith, not to say repay them. For that money was acquired by those who left it through methods which would not for a moment bear the light of this programme. And it is quite possible that, in the old foundations, some of it came from the slave trade, or from commerce to which the door was opened only by war, and war not always so scrupulous as it is now made (out of Germany). It means that the abettors of this programme should refuse (unless they are to live upon the immorality of others) all the benefits they enjoy from the history they inherit and the society in which they move. It means that they should turn monks in a Thebaid, embark for some lone island, or squat on any wild space they may find left in tracts yet unexplored. They could not from there even work their propaganda, as they must not use the post. Of course, the thing has been tried, at Oneida Creek and elsewhere, and come to grief every time. The love lacked the grace, the 'bite,' the conscience more concerned for God's holiness than for itself, the diamond edge which alone can master human nature. And this is but another of the idealisms, symptomatic of a capacious unfamiliarity with history and inexperience in affairs, and dowered with a plentiful lack of moral insight, both into the nature of evil, and, by consequence, into the nature of redemptive good. It is a *reductio ad absurdum* of certain tendencies which have captured a whole side of Christianity, and which the present crisis reveals as charming in a calm but futile for a storm. Did Lincoln not tell of the boy that got at the captain conning his steamer through the rapids, and begged him to stop the ship as his sweetest and rosiest apple had gone over the side? We are enabled to see where these drifts were leading us, not only in respect of trivialising our social life and sapping our national manhood but also in respect to the Gospel itself; whose message is blanched, its historic verve erased, its majesty of righteousness belied, its tragedy glozed, and its love made less than the costliest thing in all the world.

CHAPTER IV

JUDGMENT BY THE SAINTS

THE programme that I have just been discussing will seem to many people whose company one would like to have an engaging one; and they wonder that exception should be taken to it by any but captious polemists. Nor could exception be taken, if a New Testament revelation did not exist to trouble Israel. Its stumbling-block is one over which we are constantly falling. It is the Cross of Christ, as the apostles understood it and their writings preach it.

But, we are answered here, why drag in the Cross? This is not a matter of theology but of ethic. For the theology of our salvation the Cross may have supreme value, but this concerns the manner of our sanctification, the conduct of the saved; and our guide there is not the Cross of Christ but His teaching. The teaching of Christ is the foundation of Christian ethic. If we are asking, 'What must I do to be saved?' the reference to the Cross may be in place, but it is to the teaching of Christ we must go when we ask, 'What should I do when I am saved?'

To which the reply is manifold. The first is

that this is not what the Epistles fall back on as the source of their moral precepts. The writers make their own precepts in the main, out of the faith which the Cross created in them. Again, a religion whose moral foundation is precept cannot be a universal or eternal religion. For precepts, to be of any use, must apply first to a particular set of circumstances and a particular stage of development. They have no meaning otherwise. But, in the growth of the soul or of society, they become obsolete, and, being made for one age, they cannot be a guide for all. Even if the principle be distilled out of the precept its strength and imperative is apt to evaporate in the process. But, putting aside other objections to the position I name, there is this. The severance of the Cross as the centre of salvation from the teaching as the centre of ethic seems to canonise a distinction most fatal to the soul, and especially the social soul—the separation of religion from morality, with all its peril of a double life. The unity of Christ's mind and person forbids us to disparage His teaching in contrast with His Cross; it only drives us to interpret the teaching by the Cross where His whole person and purpose was gathered up in a final way. For a religion like Christianity, also, which unites the whole man in a reconciliation with God, there must be but one centre—the conscience, now no more divided and rent; and for that moral soul, in a religion of moral redemption, the centre can be but Christ crucified. In a religion moral above all else the centre of salvation must be the moral centre. But the centre of salvation is the Cross. The teaching therefore of Christ Himself must be interpreted by the Cross and not the Cross by the teaching. *Finis coronat opus.*[1]

The most common form of the displacement I name is not a flat choice between Word and Cross, but a reduction of the Cross to be but the chief teaching of Christ on the love of God, and no more. To rest our religion on the teaching of Christ is to reduce His Cross to a part (though the most impressive part) of that teaching. It becomes the grand exhortation or invitation uttered from God, instead of His one Redemption done. It is presented as the great object-lesson of love by sacrifice, at the cost of the achievement of the Holy One for righteousness. About the moral quality of the love or the sacrifice less is said. It is taken for granted that love, as the heart kindles to it, is the supreme good, and that sacrifice is a precious and ethical thing in itself, whose greatness is to be measured by its success in carrying home love, and giving it a moral quality which raises it above mere enjoyment. It is supposed that love is good if it is intense enough to produce sacrifice; and sacrifice is good if it is powerful enough to impress us with love. But of the moral quality intrinsic to love, as holy, apart from its form as sacrifice, and distinct from its mere quantity or intensity, little is said. As if sacrifice were the moral interior of love, and not sanctity, not righteousness, not holiness. But in itself sacrifice does not give love its moral quality. In itself it is morally neuter. It can also be the servant of unrighteousness. We may but sacrifice a less egoism to a greater. Every value in life may be sacrificed to acquisition.

[1] See Addendum at the close of this chapter.

A passionate though illicit love is capable of sacrifice which gives up both life, ease, and honour—capable in this of a greater amount of sacrifice than many make who are good and decent Christians. We have not in a sacrificial exhibition of love any necessary revelation of its moral quality as holy love, and therefore of its eternity. We must know to whom or to what the sacrifice is made. We have not through sacrifice alone *holy* love. And it was holy love that Christ came to reveal. We need the note of righteousness, and, in the case of religion, righteousness able to establish itself for ever on the universal scale.

With a revelation which did not go beyond sacrificial love we could not be sure that it was God's love or that it was eternal. We could not be sure that love was the last reality, with the reversion and dominion of all things for ever. For that we need something done and not merely shown, not merely taught. The last enemy must be destroyed, which is Love's death. Sin is action, and the confidence which it destroys only action can repair. Reality is action and not essence. It is energy and not mere disposition. It is righteousness and not piety. If it be love it is a love that *does* something, and does it on the eternal scale. It not only gives up something but gives it up for a holy purpose. It sets up an everlasting kingdom, it does not simply produce a boundless devotion. For the Kingdom of God, which was the first interest even in Christ's teaching, something must be *done* and not merely said. It was not a school, nor a group, nor a synagogue, but a matter of public affairs. And the supreme work of Christ for it was in kind. It was redemptive action, and not impressive instruction or edification.

The Cross, if Christ was perfected in it, must have consummated an element so prime and vital to Christ's teaching as the Kingdom. The very darkness that gathered round it turned it from light to power. The ruling idea of the Bible in Christ's hands had been righteousness, and not religious knowledge; and righteousness is something done. Now in the teaching of Christ nothing was done, in the strict sense of that word. The greatest of guides is not yet the King of kings. And if the Cross but continued the teaching in another and enacted form there is still nothing done. But that is not enough, we have seen, for a moral religion. Its creative revelation must be an achievement. To create is the greatest of all achievements. In the Cross, therefore, there must be more than the most impressive object-lesson; there must be the great stroke and final victory. There must be done the one thing needful for God's righteousness. In course of which *judgment* must be done on evil, in the course of the new creation of good. And it must be done in history, in the context and manner of history.

Christianity, taken with final seriousness, is a new creation. It is a new moral creation, whose historic obverse is judgment, or the reaction of holiness upon evil in the course of establishing itself in positive goodness. Divine sacrifice is not, then, sacrifice for its own sake, for morally sacrifice is neuter; nor is it just to show how great the love is, for no mere intensity makes love divine. Nor is sacrifice divine even when it meets the desires, or even the needs, of the loved. But divine sacrifice is that which considers righteousness, and meets first of all the need and nature of God's holiness in His love. It is that which meets first His holy purpose in the situation created for that love by man's sin, and in so doing inflicts historic judgment on the evil power and its agents. It is sacrifice made to God before it is offered to man. We have recently done much that was overdue to connect love with sacrifice. I will not say we have done too much of that; but we have done too little to connect it with judgment, with righteousness, with holiness. And in consequence the idea has sunk and softened—both of sacrifice and of love. Sacrifice, when it would reveal holy love, has more to do than declare it. It must meet its active demand at any cost—first by righteousness, then, in course thereof, by judgment. For all righteousness done is also a judgment on the world or the devil that resists it. Christ, in honouring the judgment of God by bearing it with its own holiness, passed judgment on Satan and on the world. Righteous sacrifice, therefore, must both atone and judge. It must hasten to hallow the holy name in action and not simply in word—in giving judgment effect and not simply expression. At any cost this must be done, unless this holiness be but a negotiable thing, and salvation a mere compromise. It must be done at the cost even of the Cross of the Son of God, Who is more than all man's life and happiness, and Who came to justify not only the conscience of man but the conscience of God, establishing love's judging and saving righteousness on the earth.

Therefore if Christian ethic deals with Christian action, and teaching is not action in the final sense, the root of Christian ethic is identical with the active, creative root of Christian faith and life. It is centred in the Cross of Christ as the eternal principle and authority for all occasional precept. And not only so. From its intrinsically holy nature, its note of righteousness, the Cross of Christ contains and deifies the element of judgment. Righteousness is its first charge—and God's righteousness, holy righteousness. It was above all else something done in love for the holiness of God, both positively in setting up His Kingdom in Christ's holy soul triumphant and universal, and negatively in destroying the Kingdom of evil. So for Christian ethic, for a life of communion with God active and not only sympathetic, the element of judgment is at least as cardinal as the element of service, and it may prescribe the form of service; we may serve Christ as the whip in His hand. It is judgment working also in the long course of history, with human agents and human conditions, since the redemptive compendium of judgment on the Cross was on the Cross of the Incarnate. It was the work of God in a true and real and historic humanity.

It is worth while to reflect on this. For one of the chief pleas of the pacifist bystanders of history is that, while judgment is not denied to work in the course of history, it can be inflicted by God alone, and man has no right to assume this tremendous function, even in God's name and service. But if

Christ may, and if Christ's Incarnation in man was real and thorough then man may and must. It is quite true man may not asume it. No man may take this office to himself, only those who are appointed thereto. But if judgment be recognised as a vital function of God's love with men, and if it is further recognised that in the Cross of Christ God's holy judgment of man fell on a consenting Christ as the chastisement of our peace, then Christ became thereby the judge of all men. And in proportion as mankind becomes the New Humanity, in proportion as Christ has His way with it, in proportion as it changes from egoism to the principle of public righteousness, in proportion as Christ thus indwells in the New Humanity and the true Church—then, in that proportion such humanity becomes the agent of His function and purpose. For, if that be not so, then the Incarnation was incomplete, and Christ cannot find or expect in human nature, however moral, a body or organ for His will. The human nature He took was then something quite different from anything possible in historic humanity, something it can never grow to. But that cannot be so. If He fully entered, and enters, a real historic humanity, the judgment right of Christ may be carried out by a solemn function of man in proportion as man is identified with His principles of society. For it is not man that then works but Christ that dwelleth in him, wherever a soul or a people seeks to moral liberty, justice, and fraternity. If man may not execute God's judgments there is an end of a moral providence in history, which can then work but by earthquake, pestilence, or famine, which are non-moral.

And if objection be raised at a point further back, where it was said that Christ, by accepting the judgment of the Cross, became the judge of all men, this is to be added to what I said a little ago about the judging action of all goodness upon the world. That action is the greater if the goodness be so good that it is crucified. If Christ bore all judgment, He became the judge of all. It was the judgment of all that He bore. If the phrase were allowed, He became our sole creditor. He bought up (if again such a phrase were permitted) all our debts, bought out every other claim, and with Him alone we have to do. To have borne our judgment gave him the sole judgment right over us. He became our Judge Who is our King. But then His Kingdom must be His agent. It must carry out His purpose. Do not let the devotional idea of sanctity exhaust the meaning of the word ; as if holiness were but prayer to God and not action for Him on men. As entire Saints men would be fully indwelt by the Judge of the earth. And in the degree in which they are the servants of His order of righteousness and stand for His righteous purpose and procedure, they are His agents in affairs —if the world's history is the world's judgment at all. This is irrespective of their complete attainment in the way of sanctity. The 'Saints' in the New Testament are not the holy, but those who have been chosen by the Holy, and ear-marked for His purpose. Were it quite certain that a particular course for one nation against another was part of the righteousness of Christ in His historic Kingdom, there could be no doubt that that nation's chastisement of the other was the judgment of God on it. But can that ever be certain? What sceptical humility! If we can never be sure that a nation's particular action in history is the exercise of Christ's righteousness, what is the worth of a nation's conscience or of its Christian name? And if there be no national conscience, then Christianity is but a private affair; there is no national righteousness, and we are where the Germans are. The German Socialists were quite German in this. Religion, they said, is *Privatsache*. The Kaiser only takes that principle in world earnest. And German Socialism, by its irreligion, is the broken reed it has shown itself to be. It is much more German than Christian or humane. (America it were wiser perhaps not to discuss.) But to exercise the judgment of Christ is part of the Christianity of the New Humanity, which is much more than a mere waiter upon Providence. It is a commissioner of the Kingdom of God, if that Kingdom rise above an individual pietism and its combinations. If a society is necessary for the moral existence of the individual, then to question the power of that society to discern God's will for it in His service is to go on to doubt the same power for the individual faith and for the concrete world.

I am bound to admit that all I have just been saying falls to the ground as a piece of speculative fantasy except on one condition. It all goes down at a breath unless it is founded on one rock. And that rock is the historic Cross as a real atonement, a real bearing of God's judgment on sin. Apart from that Christianity abjures moral history and sinks into the sand as a benevolent but ineffectual pacifism. All turns on the Cross as offered in history to God before man, offered to God's holiness more even than to man's need. It means the Cross viewed as above all else the self-hallowing of God's holy name of Love by Grace to sin under the conditions of judgment, and not merely as Love's manifestation to move men, to melt them to repentance, and infect them with sacrifice. It is the Cross as Love in judgment and not in sacrifice alone, as the acme not of the intensest Love but of the holiest, as the supreme Act of righteousness by the Kingdom's King (the crucial Act of His Reign), and not simply an act of kindness by the Head of the human family. If such a view of the Cross be but a theological figment, planted by the Apostles on a crude and uncritical Church, and hung round its neck for now two thousand years ; if such a Christ of gracious judgment do not indwell in the Church, in the world as it takes the ethic of the Church's Gospel, and in a nation as it turns from the bad old buccaneering way to the way of help, service, and justice; then all I say is but that figment elaborated, that figment in filigree. But if the Apostles were right, if they were for the revelation of Christ what He was for the revelation of God, if they not only showed Him but gave Him effect in the preached prolongation of this supreme deed, then the place of a theology of righteous judgment in a moral world and in a religion of its redemption is fundamental. Such a theology moulds ethic for Christian thought and life. Such a Cross as I press is the genetic centre of a universal ethic. And the larger life is, the Cross claims it the more. Thus the right of a Christian nation to be God's judgment on another rests on a certain view of the Atonement as the moral key and principle of the Incarnation, of the deep action of Christ in human nature, and His conquest of its history for the Kingdom of God. The resentment against the claim of theology is really against a metaphysical theology forced on the general public. But for the general soul morality is everything, and theology is the exposition of the morality of the Holy. And the sounder complaint is, not that religion should be theological, but that its theology has lost the moral note which alone gives it power for the conscience, and so command in affairs. The complaint is not without justice that some theology, and some devout theology, has done more to cosset conscience than to hallow righteousness, and to deify Love as a subjectivity than to magnify it as the sanctity eternal.

ADDENDUM ON RELIGION AND ETHIC

We do not now speak of justification and sanctification. But that is only because we are word-shy. We do talk of the things, only in a more superficial way. We speak of religion and ethic. People will read about religion and morality who will not look at anything under the title of justification and sanctification. They believe they are modern, and they are but meagre.

But now that we have called them names in a healthy, brotherly way, let us be meagre too, and talk small. We won't speak of redemption (though it is the only kind of religion of any moral use for the inner failures we really know ourselves to be when we are *chez nous*). And we won't talk of sanctification (though it is the only thing for people who are sick of their efforts at improvement). Let us tune down. Let us not seem Olympian. Let us speak of religion.

How are they related? Mostly we think of them as two different things, which we have to co-ordinate somehow (though there are some who identify them). We treat them as having a different object, or as being different functions of the soul. Religion is thought of as passive, as receptive to God, ethic as active and effective on the world. But how then about the unity of the soul, which means its peace on the one hand and its full effect on the other? There seems to be suggested a dichotomy of the person, which, in risking its unity, endangers both the ethic and the religion.

Take the case of prayer. That is our inmost and most religious hour. But if we say it is only the action of the alone with the Alone we rob it of some of its value. For it is more than that. Even there we are not lifted clean out of our moral context. Prayer is at the same moment one of the forms of our constant warfare with a stifling world, of our conquest of a crushing universe. Or, again, our daily duty. Does that win in value and power if we cut it off from every spiritual aspect, every mystic reference, and treat it but as a piece of ethic, a fidelity to our vocation, a due service of our station and calling in life? Is our active life not much coloured and shaped by our passive? Are there not certain active duties, otherwise optional, which are prescribed by our receptive relation to God?

There are three ways, I have hinted, of regarding these co-relatives, religion and ethic. They may be treated as co-ordinate, or as identical, or as reciprocal.

Take the co-ordination first. Are they but parallel?

Suppose we say they are parallel. As they are co-relative, that cannot mean that they are separable, and are neutral to each other; for it would destroy the unity of the person. What, then, is the connection? It may be causal—and causal in either direction. Either the religion produces the ethic, or the ethic the religion.

If we say that religion produces ethic, we mean that the morality springs from our relation to God as mere power or mere love—only not as holy. For that would be postulating morality in advance of its production, and the religion would not be producing it but only conveying it. Or else it would be making the morality less than pure by introducing a pre-moral, a non-moral element (power or love). It sets up in morals a heteronomy. Conscience is ruled by something other than conscience, something below it.

If we move in the other direction, and say that ethic produces religion, is that quite fair to religion? Does it not make our sense of relation to God, our faith in God, an inference from our moral achievement? Does it not make our religious certainty to rise from our moral success? And is that not a total subversion of the finest religion, certainly of our Christian religion. For such religion reveals our relation to God to be fundamentally one of refuge and rescue from our moral failure, of our need and His boon in our moral extremity. Morality is something more than a sane and Stoic life according to a moral order. It is more than a life lived according to our true moral nature. It is life where our moral nature has gone to pieces from neglect, contempt, or violence. If we are to deal with man's actual situation—the situation he admits when he is cornered, candid, and confidential—the moral life is something with a more tragic note than the Stoics feel or the young mystics who go round as the soul's piano-tuners to the Infinite. The centre, source, and standard of our morality is not a moral order but a moral crisis. It is not philosophic but historic. The actual conscience (in the individual at least), being so near to the miracle of the will's freedom, has fundamentally to do with a crisis in which it is saved, and not with a culture in which it is schooled. I wish we had more moral schooling in our culture. But the root matter is a regeneration and not simply an ethical rehabilitation, nor even a moral renaissance.

But if the one do not spring from the other in a way exactly *causal*, if the morality is not just the effect of the religion, is it this way? Is the religion, the faith in God, just a *postulate* of morality, a condition of ethic? The defect in that view is that it makes us most sure of God when we need Him least—at the height of our moral success and satisfaction—as our Patron or our Rewarder. In the depth of our failure and distress God as a moral postulate is neither very apparent nor very useful. We need Him most as a Saviour, not a Rewarder. And does this not affect the purity of the ethic, and the love of good for its own sake—to say nothing of its misreading of our actual moral position and need.

Let us now suppose that religion and ethic are identical—that they are not co-ordinated either as cause or postulate, but are the same. This would lead some to think of a mystic morality, and others to think of a legalist religion. We have either a mystic morality leading to pride or slackness, or we have an exigent religion leading to despair. On the one hand the soul feels itself identical with the deity. That means that everything that hampers the Ego is regarded as an unworthy limitation of the Almighty of which the self is a phase. Every such thing must be resented and overridden. Or else the obstacle is a limitation in the Deity Himself that cannot be removed; it is a fate or process. It is then a source of Oriental resignation and indifference. On the other hand we have a legalist religion, a religion only on terms of prescriptive ethic, which grows in complexity, with the enlargement of life, to an intolerable burden; or where each crime severs from God, and the offender in one point is exposed to all the 'curse of the Law.' Whose end in either case is despair.

As a matter of fact religion and ethic can be neither severed nor identified any more than the two cusps of the arch. Nor is the stability of the arch a matter of compromise. There is both distinction and identity between them. They balance and sustain each other. If they are not causal to each other, nor the same, they are reciprocal. But what does that mean? Does it not mean that both arise from a fact which contains both, requires both, creates both? Does it not mean that the source of both is at once moral in nature and religious in power? And is there any such source known to us except the fact of Christ in His atoning life and death, Christ Whose judgment grace is the crisis of the moral Universe, Who is at once the criterion of all ethic in His holy Act and in His love the Saviour from that curse of despair which waits upon our moral failure. He is our righteousness and our Redeemer. In the same One Person and Act we have the source of both ethic and religion. We have the mystic Christ *in us* identical with the moral Christ *for us*. 'I live, yet not I but Christ in me.' 'Without Me ye can do nothing.' His sacrifice was morally perfect else it could not be atoning to a holy God, and it also stands over us as a transcendent Redemption. With His moral perfection He dwells in us sinners; and in virtue of the same He is our propitiation. His justification is also our sanctification. He is the object both of our religion (which is faith in Him) and of our ethic (which is done to Him more even than to the least of His whom we help and serve).

CHAPTER V

PASSIVE RESISTANCE

THE question arises how far those are justified in Christian ethic whose peace principles would lead them to a passive resistance in the event of compulsory service. Passive resistance is a dangerous weapon, far too dangerous for the young and crude; and the more so that it is almost impossible to prevent its use by improper persons. But these considerations may not be without force.

Passive resistance to the State for Christian reasons is less a matter of individual and private conscience than of duty on the Church. But on the Church the duty may lie on due occasion; let the individual convert the Church to his view. 'The supreme institution of political life, the State, is not sovereign; in the sense that, when a man's allegiance is divided between what he owes to the State and what he owes to some other social institution, it does not follow that State allegiance must be recognised as supreme' (Delisle Burns). There is a sovereign society above the State, though it may be less obvious, and though it should be described as an organism rather than an organisation. And any Christian protest or refusal as against the State should be in the name and service of this

Church and its trust, and not merely on the ground of natural ties or instincts (as in the revolt of Antigone), nor on the plea of individual convictions alone. I am not saying that refusal would never be justified in such cases if they became extreme, only that it would not then be religious, it would not be on the ground and imperative of an ethic distinctively Christian. But, on whatever ground, unlimited liberty to any individualism that calls itself conscience, even in a Christian man, is an impossible thing, because it is sheer atomism, ending in self-will; and it is ruinous to a community—which, as the supremacy of the Kingdom of God shows, is the first Christian consideration. If the Christian is to resist the State in this way it must be on the ground of some action by the State which imperils or destroys the foundation of the Church's life, and is by an autonomous Church felt to do so. Loyalty to Church or State is the form in which loyalty to conscience is most safe and effective. The matter of our chief choice is which is to be supreme.

What then is the foundation and principle of the Church's life? It is a religion and not an ethic. It is the faith and worship of the Saviour; it is not obedience to a legislator, even were he the supreme prophet. It is no matter of applied ethics, but the soul's moral regeneration by a Redeemer. It is the faith and worship of a Redeemer. His supreme work was indeed the core, the crisis, and the crown of all the moral spirit of the universe. The Cross of Christ was the foundation not of a faith only but of an ethic intrinsic to it, and not less than cosmic. Only it was not the publication of an ethical code, and its note is not mere amendment. Its ethic was creative of soul, it was not regulative of conduct. It was evangelical and not legal. It was regenerative and not prescriptive. It said, love with the new love and do as you like. The prescriptive element in Christianity belonged to the valuable rather than the vital, and it might be but occasional and temporary in its form. It was less grace than guidance. It belonged to the *bene esse* of the Church and not its *esse*. The Church is not an ethical society, therefore an ethical issue should not rend it. The ethical form is a real, but it is a derivative, feature in it. Its faith and its works are inseparable, but they do not rank alike. The faith produces the work, and not the work the faith. The fixed faith produces variable work according to time and place. The many works reflect the one faith, they are not alternative to it, they are not in a parity with it. The foundation of the Church is the Gospel, as regenerative for the soul, it is not the Sermon on the Mount, as directive for conduct. The teaching was guidance for those who already were new made by the Gospel, and it is only practicable in any shape by those who possess that supernatural power. It expresses the principle between brothers and not mere neighbours, between Christians; it has not nations in view as the Cross has; and it can hold between nations only in so far as they are composed of real Christians. The practical forms of the Christian life vary from time to time, and vary even from the precepts of the Sermon. But the Gospel which makes the Church a Church is changeless. It is the Gospel of the grace of God, and the loving power of His saving righteousness in the Cross of Christ. For the Church that is central and constitutive, but the conduct of its affairs, the fruits of the Spirit, are more peripheral and regulative. The relation of the Church to its Redeemer is fixed, but within that allegiance its relations with men vary. The Gospel does not vary, but its moral applications do. And, as a matter of fact, we find within the Church catholic much diversity of view, among people equally entitled to an opinion, about applied Christianity, but we have no diversity about the Gospel as fixing the relation between God and man, the Saviour and the soul. One Lord, one faith, but operations many. One power and principle of the Spirit, but much flexibility of precept according to occasion. So that the Epistles do not use the code of Christ but make their own injunctions—some of which need considerable adjustment to Christ's, such as the deliverance of So-and-so to Satan as a mode of loving him. To obey Christ is an ambiguous phrase, and its obvious sense is its inferior. It means first of all to obey Him as Redeemer, to make the surrender a Redeemer calls for, to take His forgiving and regenerating grace in living faith more even than to toil after His manner of conduct. It is to submit to His sure salvation more even than to comply with His palpable precepts. It is to worship the Saviour absolutely and be ready to obey whatever He unmistakably enjoins rather than to obey commands at their face value while we keep back part of our soul from His Redemption. The Church at least rests on His Redemption and not His injunction.

The point is that for the Church (which, and not

sporadic or atomic Christians, is here the main concern) the central and creative thing is its Gospel, relating it to Christ, and not its Ethic, relating it to man. Its Ethic has a relation to the State, its Gospel has none except through its Ethic. The public and business form of love is righteousness. Thus if anything so grave is to be undertaken by Christian people as resistance to the State which they have a free citizen's power to influence and alter, it can only be justified as in the vital interest of something so great as the Church, and not of the atomic conscience. It should be an expression of the social conscience of the Church concerning an invasion of that which forms the very life and unity of the Church. And what forms the Church's life is the Gospel, concerning which we can be much more sure, and therefore strong, than we can be concerning any one of its ethical applications. For in the one case we have our certainty direct from Christ in the Spirit, and in the other we have it as an act of our Christian judgment, more or less educated by the past, upon a situation—unless of course we bring down Christ from a Redeemer to a legislator, and reduce the report of His precepts for His first group to cast-iron imperatives for all time.

The result of these considerations is that if the State requires of us conduct incompatible with the love and worship of Christ as Redeemer it strikes at the existence of the Church and must be resisted. Such an issue was presented to the early Church by the demand from Christian soldiers of the military oath, which was objected to less on the grounds of the Sermon on the Mount than because it involved a confession of the Emperor's deity inconsistent with the place of Christ in His Gospel. And in a free State, where we have a free voice and action, the resistance must be more than passive and private. It should be active and concerted, for the Gospel, as I say, is not a matter of the lone conscience and the free lance. The resister should be the Church, and not the individual except as a member of the Church; who should feel that he had done his duty in a protest as forcible as possible short of rebellion when worship is not involved.

But when it is a question not of Christian Gospel and worship but of Christian ethic, i.e. of the application of the moral principle of the Christian Cross to an actual and practical situation, then, since the centrality and certainty are less in this region, since so much depends on our facts and our judgment, there is not the same right or duty to resist a discussed and deliberate ordinance of the State concerning *its* life. For the State is an ethical institute of God for us as much as the family is, and it is in its way equally, though less obviously, powerful for our moral growth. In this regard it is inferior only to the Church. 'In a list we might make of all human beings the dead far outnumber the living; and the effects of their thought and action are much more important politically than the thought and action of all the living put together.' 'More and more,' says Comte, 'the dead rule us.' And the longer history is the more weighty it is. Hence, from what was said in the last paragraph, the Church's right to resist the State in the ethical region would be in proportion as its conviction on the point raised approached the unanimity of its worship of Christ. For instance, there would be no doubt as to the Church's unanimity, and the individual Christian's right to resist, if the State commanded any of its members to assassinate the Kaiser, or if it encouraged any in promiscuous intercourse for the purpose of restocking the population. For these traverse the very nature of right, which it is the real business of war to restore.

The Christian duty to the State becomes doubly and trebly urgent when that State is not only fighting for its life, but stakes that life in the cause of a world-righteousness and a national humanity which are vital to the Kingdom of God. For if religion was denationalised in the Cross human relations were not; and even religion was rather supernationalised. It is a question worth asking ourselves whether the present concern of the Founder of that Kingdom in His New Covenant is exclusively with the lenitives of war, as if He were the divinest of all Franciscans, and not, as the Lord's Messiah, with the righteous issue joined between peoples reckoned as something else than crowds. It is a question whether He, Who is certainly with the ambulance, is not with equal certainty in the heart of the moral fray of nations, and the King, Marshal, and Judge of His Kingdom there. Is Christ but the King of saints and not the King of kings?

If such considerations have any bearing on the *subjects* of pacifist resistance, what are we to say as to the action of the *object* of it, the Government? To many people such resisters will seem but cranks, and it may be feared they find but short shrift with some tribunals. No doubt also among the recalcitrants there may be several who are cranks—which may be said of many causes that pass for more respectable. But liberty is not a positive principle; nor is principle the clue it should be in perplexity, if it do not give us room, and even some tenderness, for those who tax it most. The honest exercise of conscience is a thing so precious that we may well be more willing that liberty should be strained by the perverse amateur conscience than that even these trying people should be repressed. We have reason to be thankful for the very extravagances of our freedom in this country, and reckon them cheap at the price, when we see what the total absence of political liberty, or free opinion, and the policing of cranks has cost Germany, and, through her, the world. Much consideration should be shown in any legislation, or other action, towards those with whom we have some ground to be impatient. We have claimed just and considerate treatment from the State when our Free Churches were outwardly but sects like first century Christianity; let us use the same treatment towards those national sectaries—until at least they propose, or promise, to take command of the situation, and leave the national life to be pulverised for good by an enemy who in his victory would have no mercy. None can now doubt that he would be merciless but a good nature too credulous to discern spirits, or too limited to gauge the actual situation.

CHAPTER VI

THE MORAL SANCTION OF FORCE

THE question of Force and Morals is naturally one that exercises more people than usual at a time like the present. It is pressed upon every mind in the crisis of a world war. But not only so. It is an urgent aspect of the most vast and permanent conflict of the whole world, of the issue of Nature and Grace. In language still more theological (as all the final issues tend to be) it is the question how a cosmic Redemption subdues to its uses all the powers of the world. It is not wonderful therefore that there should be much difference of opinion, and much perplexity that cannot settle to an opinion. What is wonderful is the promptness and the confidence with which so many settle problems of the kind by a swift appeal to what they call the simplicities of a young intuition or an ancient precept.

The question is not really one of the presence of force in moral action but of its prevalence, its domination. Force is there, in the world where conscience has to act. It must be reckoned with in life and practice. We can retire to no region where it does not work, either in us or through us. It must even be used by us. The only question then is whether it shall at last use the conscience or be used by it, whether it shall dominate or serve moral ends.

For religious people that question would seem to be settled by the fact that God uses it. By His ordinance we conquer nature and its forces by obeying them. Coercion even is part of His method. He compels the most unwilling by physical force to quit life. His very Grace works by way of outward judgment. Corporeal penalty is in His merciful providence. Love chastises, and chastises with something else than the sting of conscience alone. Every headache after a debauch is a divine use of force. Every paralysis after years of debauch is but the extension of the same principle. Every nation that goes to hell in blood and flame for forgetting God extends the application farther. The dreadful power to take up weapons against the Kingdom of God is yet from God. 'Thou couldest have no power against me except it were given thee from above.'

It is impossible to deny that the holy God, Who means a Kingdom of righteousness, uses force for the moral purposes of that holiness in its stages among men. The only exit from this is to say that God has not entrusted to men the agency of this action. God (it is said) inflicts judgment but does not allow weak and evil men to be His deputies in the infliction. He is His own executioner. Natural process may be His servant in this matter but not civil. A fit might punish crime, but not a rope. The murderer's gun might burst but we must not shoot him. A convulsion of nature (where no nemesis can be traced) might serve God's moral will but not a convulsion of nations (where it can). That belongs to fallen nature which is no more God's minister. But such a position goes farther than even the thoroughgoing Reformers went when they left the *justitia civilis* in corrupt man as still a relic and monument of a divine humanity. It seems to be part of the wide conspiracy to belittle man and his moral trust, to take the greatness out of conscience even in its ruins, and to give its finest conflicts no more moral value than we might assign to an earthquake, with no contribution to the coming of the Kingdom. And that descends at last to a mere Naturalism. It drives us to seek any revelation we may have of the Great Power's intent only in the region of Nature with its force and process, and not in the conscience of history, of free man. To this result comes the conscience amateur and scrupulous. That is the end of a pedestrian, a burgher, ethic, without the grand style but with the meddling habit. It is a morality that cannot float. It destroys itself. It works out to the denial of anything more than natural process. Or, if it keep the idea of a revelation, it is a revelation only in an antiquated sense —by way of physical miracle. It does not give us a true supernatural but only a preternatural, a revelation which, by deposing conscience as the agent of God, loses the moral in the miraculous.

That is what I do if I do not resist evil but leave God to intervene if He wants it resisted. I leave Him to take moral responsibility, I take none. Conscience is not His vicar. *He* must strike the ravisher dead. *He* must paralyse the murderer's arm. *He* must send legions of angels if He wishes the invader withstood. If He send no such reinforcements He does not wish resistance. Satan, indeed, has no hesitation about force, nor have his earthly angels; but he may only be met by Michael, not by England. It is really moral fatalism, or at best crude despotism. It crushes moral action. As a matter of fact He rarely so intervenes. Still He might. Thus the end of this creed could only be to demoralise life in the way gambling does—to destroy a faith in order or in anything we could rely on, and to make life jumpy. We look to the incalculable, and trust neuropathic visions in the clouds more than serried conscience on the field. And in the very last we should believe not even in faith but in freak, and call it piety. The expectation of miracle is really fatal to *morale.* We may believe in miracles but we may not rely on them, we may not expect them. They have a purpose, but we are not to trade on them. They are gifts in life but not guides—just as we welcome the genius but do not wait for him. We are not to jump from pinnacles in the faith that an unseen hand will arrest us, buoy us, and make us float down through the air upon the gaping crowd, to be hailed as the real Messiah. It is all part of a wide scepticism and impatience of law, in which the extreme pacifist and the anarchist join hands. But we are to *overcome* evil, and to do it with good, with positive good, with moral good relevant to it, with the good it is entitled to. We do not overcome it by simply turning away to cultivate some good frame of mind, or to do some good of a quite irrelevant kind, and by taking our stab in the back. It is often thought that by sacrifice we can evade duty; but it is false religion. It is *corban.* The patience of the saints is not there to act simply as moral spectacle, a piece of impressionism melting the spectators, or making the soldiers fall back. It is to have its *perfect work;* it meets evil with judgment, not with mere retaliation; it meets passion not with passion but law. The patience of the saints is not melodramatic, smiling down fear to show how a Christian can die. It is the patience of power, co-operating with an active God, and not lying down, nor turning aside from an imperative conflict to a pious quietism or an optional and self-chosen philanthropy.

So far as all experience goes, society is quite necessary for morality, and force is quite necessary for society, if it be but to prepare its own disuse. We must only see that it is a means and not a foundation. It is a schoolmaster, a tutor, and not a great teacher sent from God. Society must use force but it does not rest on it. The basis of society is law or right, whether formal or informal. Faith in law is the great prophylactic of war. And the only true object of war is to restore law to its place. It is not really the policeman that keeps order; the law does, and the spirit of law which put him there. If the policeman is not backed by the law society turns on him, and by lawful force deposes him. But if it could not put him there it would not be law. Law would not be law if it *could* not use force. It would be unable to make its authority real. It would not have its home where Hooker saw it—in the very bosom of the Holy and Almighty. It would be authoritative only where its authority was not needed, only with people already sympathetic, already in tune with it.

'Yes,' it is said, 'that is the true state of things. Love can dispense with law.' Now it is not quite easy to be patient with such dreamers—unless they are very nice indeed, which many of them are, and some are not superior at all and have no moral 'side.' But, in the first place, love does not dispense with law. The supreme revelation of love in Christ's Cross came by the magnifying of law and its honouring. Divine love is always holy love, and for God there is a law of holiness, i.e. of absolute righteousness, always tonic within the atmosphere of love. Law is enthroned in the very heart of the God of Love—if we have any faith left in a Revelation by Atonement. Love without law (and law that can make itself good) is but double-barrelled egoism. Christianity is not the religion of Love but of holy Love Omnipotent. For love, however ideal, might be helpless in the face of its last defiance. Christianity is the religion of the omnipotence of Love in forgiving and reclaiming its last enemy. It is the religion of that in love which insures its final and universal reign. It is the religion of holy Love and of moral Redemption.

> For when the power of imparting good
> Is equal to the will, the human soul
> Requires no other heaven.

Christianity is a religion not of love only but of power. Its cross is the world Act not of love alone but of its moral conquest of all things.

And, in the second place, it is not with heaven that history has yet to do, or a historic God. It is remarkable in such times as these how a taste for grandiose ideas is combined with a total lack of any sense of actual situation. Love became incarnate, and really, relevantly, organically so, among those who were yet but the trivial and the evil. Christ died dealing actively with an actual historic situation and duty. We have in the name of duty to deal with the actual, with love in a very imperfect state, and with people who know nothing of it but as egoist passion and instinctive self-will. Even where it does not challenge law and defy it, love, as we find it, is an unstable base for society. For, at its present stage, it is too much a matter of mood. At one time we are disposed in love to recognise society and act on duty, at another to ignore it and pursue our egoism. So, to protect us from that uncertainty, moral civilisation, by a process which sifts centuries, sets up laws in the interest of the many (i.e. in the name of love). It sets up law (which is right backed by might) coercing egoism, directing duty, and punishing wrong. And a very precious and costly product it has been. But that is not to say that coercion is the foundation of law or justice, nor is it the bond of society. It is a mere clamp—a golden clamp, but still a clamp; it is not a cement. It is a clamp to act till the cement really set and the union is sound. Marriage is not made without the contract, but it is not the contract that makes the marriage. A bond of that outward kind destroys society if we rest on it in chief. It substitutes for a deep, immanent, and destined unity a fundamental strife, repulsion, war. But that is not our fundamental case. My metaphor of a clamp limps. A clamp only holds two bodies that will not cohere. But that is not the deep divine nature of man. So law is more even than a cement. It is a commissure. It is the medium of educative intercourse for two or more beings that were meant to co-operate, meant for each other, and are not in fundamental antagonism. It is not the coercion for eternal strife, but the discipline of eternal love. It is a tutor, even if not a spirit of life. Right *founded* on might is indeed no right. And in proportion as it is always appealing to might, and always keeping might in evidence, it can demoralise us. It can demoralise us by reducing people to live only on the level of the things they are compelled to do. But that is not the fault of the law but of the people, of people who love and trust nobody. Law is a fence round the young plant of love to give it room to grow and to keep the brutes off. Law as force is there to repair love's weakness and not to replace its strength. Conscience is therefore not against the use of force but only against its dominion. God uses it Himself, as I have said, and it cannot be forbidden to the conscience which reflects and obeys Him, and is His fellow worker.

What creates a State is in so far like what creates a Church that it is a moral power. In the one case it is the respect for law, in the other the faith in Grace. But each is essentially a moral power (else the Cross of Grace were not a real atonement but only a piece of sacrifice; and sacrifice, even for love, *may* or *may* not be moral). The coercive power is exercised under a certain moral principle and for certain moral ends. It is *by* law *for* righteousness. There rests the coercive force of sovereignty—force ancillary to ideal and moral realities called rights. It is the State that makes the Sovereign in a free community, not the Sovereign the State. (In a Church it is otherwise. We do not choose our soul's King; He chooses us. But on that I cannot enlarge here.) The Sovereign power does not create rights but expresses and insures them. It is moral will and not force that is the basis of the State, and of the family of States living in mutual respect.

The whole question is condensed in the right of public punishment, the right of the magistrate. No doubt every man has a right to a life as free and full as by social help he can make it. And punishment is an interference with that right of freedom. But the man's right is one whose enjoyment is only secured him by social recognition. And it is recognised socially in this way in order that he may contribute to the public good. He has the right also to die on due cause; he has the duty to accept death for, and even from, his brethren who secure his life. (We do not now believe practically that death inflicts either extinction or hopeless hell, but only expulsion from earthly society.) The public has the right to prevent him at any cost from acts which interfere with the public good, and the free action of others for it. The public can withdraw its recognition of his free life, and treat him as unfree and socially dead. Society, as a moral being, must use force on such a person to save others in their right and freedom and richness of life. Force to this end is sanctioned, and even sanctified, by morality. And the culprit, as he became moral, would feel it his duty to die under that force for the public good. A free and moral life for all is the great object of society, whether as Church or as State. But it has its conditions. There are some that make it impossible. And these must be arrested or destroyed that goodness may live. If nothing else will do, such force must be used—unless we recast our idea of goodness, and call it yielding to wicked force in a piety; which is to strip religion of moral value. And that is religion's chief bane. There are cases where even war (which is force *in excelsis*) is the only means of defending this liberty and fulness of life, not for a nation only but for a world. There are cases where an international magistracy must be brought to bear, and penalty inflicted in the name of all that God has revealed as a divine humanity. Then 'the wrong of destroying physical life and arresting individual liberty disappears in the paramount right of preserving the conditions under which moral life is possessed.' Even John Bright thought there was no means but the American war to destroy the worse evil of slavery.

The moral sanction of such magisterial force should be in no lower hands than those of the nation or the nations, of the nation as representing humanity and not riding over it. In the hands of a class, force which threatens a nation is immoral. I am thinking of the general strike and its war on society. The individual certainly cannot take such law into his own hands. And the soldier does not, under his strict oath and discipline. He is (as I have already said) the agent and mandatory of his State, as that State should be of humanity. He has its commission. He is its sheriff, its executioner. This would extend even to a sharp crisis within civil and peaceful society, as the law recognises in justifiable homicide. In such a crisis the man who takes the life of the would-be murderer or ravisher is acting as the agent of the State, and is a magistrate *ad hoc*, to maintain the first condition of social life and right. He is suddenly appointed by the situation as special constable to disable the offender, but to stop him at any cost, even of life if it must be so. He is then also, for the Christian law, under cover of the principle of Romans xiii. 4. He is a minister of God for good. The life of the would-be murderer is forfeit. To prefer that he should kill rather than that he should die is immoral. We may not help the evil will to effect. Not to resist is to be accessory. It is to leave the door open for the robber. Passivity is complicity. And it is profaning Christ to use His precepts of love to erase the distinction between good and evil, freedom and crime.

A historic crisis of the first order must carry us onward not only to religion but to the very central depths and creative source of our religion. If God has committed all judgment to the incarnate Son He has committed some to the men in whom the Son works, and works more than even they know. The total repudiation of force, and especially of man's use of it, for any moral end is the mark of a wrong standard of religion and the fruit of a perverse type. It is the ethic of a religion which practically ignores the wrath of God, and finds either no real place in the Saviour for the Cross, or no place in the Cross for more than sacrifice—none for the divine judgment.

Such religion provides, therefore, no charter for the saintship that should judge the world, except in the poor sense of passing an opinion about it. The Cross is not then the supreme judgment of God in history, nor are the good 'in Christ' equipped for any such function. This creed destroys ethic because it ousts an atoning Cross, meeting in love the reaction of *holy* judgment, for one merely sacrificial or declaratory. It damages ethic because it worships a God whose love is free enough to give everything in a Saviour but not *holy* enough to require anything from Him. What shocks a certain religious temperament (rather than devout faith) is the whole element of judgment in history, whether in its course or at a point on the Cross. What repels such people from a real Atonement—which is man and God reciprocally active in judgment—staggers them also in a moral providence and their part in it. This is a religion in which the sympathetic and mystical has dislodged the ethical, and it tends to destroy Christianity as the religion of moral redemption. The inner light deepens the darkness without, and loses the signals lighted for the conscience there. And by that I keep meaning not that such a religion does not have an ethic for a sequel, but that it has reduced it to be but a sequel, and removed it from the inner nature and creative Act of the religion, as distinct from its mere results. The judgments of the holy, of the absolutely moral, God did not then fall on Christ in His Cross; nor did Christ therein judge the world in blood. The holiness which must react on sin as judgment is omitted from that notion of love. The Sovereignty has gone out of the Fatherhood. That is to say, judgment is but a device of fatherhood, it is not a positive and constituent element in fatherhood. The conceptions of love are those that come home to private, domestic, and tender experience, not those that are active on the public scale in history as righteousness. Ethic (and religion with it) ceases to be impressive because it loses the historic scale. It has personal sympathy without moral insight. There is much fineness of devout feeling and fancy, but a lack of imaginative moral realism. There is much gentleness but no sense of judgment, much simplicity and no subtle sense of divine irony. There is a lack of moral imagination of the kind that weighs the meaning of guilt, and world guilt, the kind that perceives how God used not only force but even man's abuse of force for His Redemption. There is an absence of the austere, eternal, and majestic mercy which laid on Christ the iniquity of us all. Its Kingdom of God is not first righteousness but devout affection and fraternal piety. It is not indeed too much by way of doing good, but it is too little by way of doing right; and if more people did right fewer would need doing good. With such a cross the Church is like a company in a room which groups itself about the old hearth, but all that is there is a gas fire, or a few electric bulbs tinted.

If the Cross was but suffering a martyrdom, and the Soul of Christ was but enduring force instead of mastering it and making it an offering to God, then He neither felt nor wielded the judgment of God. He did not perfectly confess that judgment just which He took, and therefore He did not acquire the right and power of judgment for the whole world.

And if this element, this supremely moral element, is removed from the spot which is the creative centre of Christian religion, then the life that rises there is severed from an intrinsic ethic, its saints cannot judge the world, and the good cannot effect God's judgment in history, but only follow certain disputed precepts of a quietist kind. The men the Cross makes cannot feel that they are called, by union with such a Cross as is left, to be Christ's assessors and agents in those judgments which distil the Kingdom of God out of history. If Christ was but passive to the will of God in His death then Christians must be passive to God's judgments in life and the world. Resignation takes the place of co-operation.

It may appear that, in the writer's view, the source of Christian ethic, when we go to the very root of the matter, is theological. That is so. In the last radicalism it is the Cross of Christ. The deep, final, and commanding ethic for the soul, the kind of ethic that has its range, not in individual, domestic, or dilettantist morality, but in the moral movement providential for generations and for ever, is theological. And it will vary according to the nature of that Act which Christian faith treats as the moral centre of its universe—the Cross, which gathered into one eternal and regenerative Act the whole and holy person of Christ. It will vary according as we recognise there the judgment of God's holy love in creative action for history, or only a lesson in divine love by a piece of sacrifice—a real Atonement, or a deep impression. The Cross of Christ is the fountain of Christian ethic, as it is of His *Holy* Spirit. The teaching of Christ, on which at present so much stress is laid (especially the Sermon), is but a series of illustrations of the power and principle of the Cross occasioned by certain circumstances. To substitute the teaching of Christ for His Cross as the ethical source, instead of using it as illustration, is a very wide and anti-evangelical error. It displaces our centre of gravity, and therefore causes Christianity to falter where it should firmly tread. It is an error parallel, in the Gospels, to that which, in the Epistles, makes the Sacraments instead of the Word the chief legacy of Christ to the Church. The whole Church needs a re-moralising, and it can only acquire it by a return upon the source of its new life as being, in the same act, its moral centre. It must re-orient itself at its own pole. The source of Christian ethic must surely be identical with the source of Christian life. It has been the bane of evangelical Christianity, and often its perdition, to have severed justification in the cross (or religion) from sanctification in the spirit (or ethic); as if each had its own source, and one section (the orthodox) took stand on the former, while another (the heretics) took stand on the latter. Whereas 'all flows from the cross and from our dying there' ('The Imitation'). What the Church needs most for the service of a world to which conscience at the long last means more than even 'heart,' what religion most needs if it is to go beyond mystic elation and be a control and guide for life, is a recoupling with that one holy current, a resettlement on that foundation of the Cross, in whatever modern terms. And there is no small hope that the war may help us in that way, and put the colour back into the blood of Christ. It may restore to piety a due sense of the element of judgment in history and at the heart of grace—judgment in the divine course of history because judgment at the divine point of history. For what repels us from a real Atonement in the blood of Christ the righteous also robs of its sanctity the blood shed in every cause of historic righteousness, and unnerves the conscience which goes to pain and death as a fellow worker with the historic judgment of God.

I am liable to be told that I may be proving too much, and that if these things are so then we should use force in aid of faith and pursue wars of religion. That will not bear a moment's reflection. It is not urged that war may be made in order to do good but to prevent the prevention of good, to resist wrong, and especially wrong to those who cannot resist for themselves. May we not peck the cat for the chickens under our wing? If words cut deeper than wounds Christ struck very fiercely at the foes of His brood. It is very certain now that religion cannot be spread by force (though it has taken the world a long time to learn it); but is faith just irrelevant to force? God, indeed, did more than judge the world in Christ's Cross; but He did judge it. Did He not use Assyria on Israel? I have spoken of A.D. 70; did He not use Rome against Jerusalem in A.D. 70? Was there no connection between the rejection of Christ and the destruction of Zion? Did Christ, as the providence of His own Kingdom, not summon then the legions it did not suit Him to ask for to avert the Cross? And religion may sympathise with the power, however imperfect, that uses force to arrest wickedness and defend liberty. The prophet who does not go into the battle may yet mean much for the soldiers and the victory. If religion forbid the fight of a State for its life, and for the moral life of the world, it is outlaw religion; and it must take the consequences of being *inimica generis humani*, as the Jews were by the Roman declared to be. It must lose not only the benefits but the confidence of the society it will not serve. And it must incur what we cannot help feeling for those who live in comfort behind the bayonets they denounce, and prosper much by a machinery defended by guns, in a society only possible by fleet and camp.

There come times when we are thrown almost into despair by the necessity of fighting over again battles which we thought were won for good and all, and on whose results we were basing our whole mental and moral world. Many had that feeling some years ago in the political world on the question of Free Trade. And such is also the case, on a far vaster scale, with the present war. We are called upon by its developments to revise some of what we thought the most settled principles of civilised society. We seem to have to begin restoring society from its moral foundations, and rebuilding humanity from its base. By a long historic evolution, coming to a head rapidly during the latter part of last century, we thought we had secured another foundation and another principle than force as the base of society. We thought force had in the main been replaced by fraternity, and that militarism had been taught its true place by law and justice. We had come to think that commerce was to put round the world a girdle of peace by reciprocal interests and mutual respect. But on a sudden all is changed. All is put on the hazard again. Force, enhanced with all the resources of natural civilisation, and justified by the repudiation of any moral obligation for States, has broken loose on mankind. Militarism is again desolating Europe. But it is not in the old form which sought the glory of a soldier genius or of a dynasty. There was a remnant of poetry and chivalry in that, as such things go. The soldier was more or less of a knight. But this is different. The huckster has taken command even of the soldier and debased him. Mammon is a more ignoble god than Mars. The passion of greed is mean compared with the passion for glory. The very commerce from which so much was hoped has become the moving source of this relapse and degradation. The creature we petted has bitten us. The snake we warmed has stung. To do the soldiers justice it is the traders that have promoted this war—with the soldiers no doubt as their willing tools. It is a war of industry. It is an economic war—everything is said now to be economic at last. It has been forced by a desperate financial situation, caused by the sudden conversion of an agricultural people to an industrial, and by the passion of a too prosperous industrialism to capture the markets of the earth for German products. The new production was forced by the French milliards; and to effect the capture these products were sold abroad at such a loss that the advertisement bill meant impending bankruptcy; and war is, among other things, a last gamble to avert it. The fate of Socialism has shown how little humane righteousness without a religion can resist mere racialism. Germany has become since 1870 a *nouveau riche*, and it keeps the parvenu's habit of mind and morals. The workman risen to be an employer is often said to be the worst of employers, the most aggressive, provocative, and brutal. He was brought up on blows, perhaps, as an apprentice, and they remain his nature, however covered. So the capable, rapid, and materialist prosperity of Germany, overleaping itself, falls on the desperate venture of war to prevent the awful collapse impending on its frenzied finance. Mere finance, without moral restraint, ends in force without methods even humane. As its field is the world it is all society that is involved; and what is at stake is the moral principles that make society worthy, to say nothing of Christian. War on a world scale is declared on the Kingdom of God by Mammon, Mars, and lying Mercury. And so society for its own safety, as for God's Kingdom, has to engage with the primitive man who neither fears God nor regards his kind. We have to cope with an egoism not only colossal but ignoble, with a passion not of ambition but of mere coarse covetousness. Prospero has to take order with Caliban. (And I am forgetting nothing of legitimate national ambitions or thorough practical power.) We have to stop, turn back, and lay again the foundations, when we should have been going on to perfection. Force must be met with force, for conscience sake, for the world's sake and the Kingdom's. But it is a case of force which repudiates moral control being met by force in the service of righteousness and humanity, by force under the principle of the Kingdom of God which is by Germany openly disavowed.

It is remarkable that a world revolution and dissolution should come from the most conservative of States. We are familiar with revolution as the negative product of an unteachable Conservatism, by way of reaction. But this is revolution led by such Conservatism. It is an egoist, military and militant, Conservatism. It is Feudalism in a long belated survival (and this is the last struggle of Feudalism). Its peace was only the equilibrium of a high explosive, it was not the stability of righteousness. Power, if morality do not wield it, only goes to pieces, like an overdriven fly-wheel. Force, without that sanction, dies of its own density, like an attack in close formation. Yet to leave force to the non-moral, to have all the moral people feeling too moral to use it against its abuse, or too proud to fight, is to make a present of it to Satan, and to leave the world to him so far as any action of ours goes. It is to become 'procuress to the Lords of Hell.' Progress is not secured by civilisation nor culture but by living and active faith in a holy God, whose judgments are deeper than all devilry and whose servants are the just and bold.

CHAPTER VII

CHRISTIAN LOVE AS PUBLIC RIGHTEOUSNESS

WHAT one misses in certain lovable types of religion is the historic sense, and an ethic upon that scale, ethic in the grand style—the sense of a cosmic righteousness and a historic continuity of public regeneration, with duty accordingly. They have the note of sympathy and the intuition of ideas, but no sense of a situation. They can picture a destiny but they cannot measure powers. They are moral artists. They dwell on what ought to be, were the world radically different from what it actually is. And especially do they fail to realise the total moral situation of the sinful world before a God of holy love and saving judgment—its salvation by fire. The war is a lightning flash which reveals the fundamental difference, slumbering unborn in the heart of peace, between the twin types of religion—one of the naïve heart and one of the freed conscience; one Esau, one Jacob; one genial, one holy; one lovable to his kind, one elect for the world; one (pious and sympathetic) dwelling on the blessing of God's fatherly love, and the other (moral and evangelical) living on the grace of justification by faith; one asking sweetly for 'Lead, kindly light,' the other humbly for 'Rock of Ages'; one engrossed with the mystic soul, the other with a mystic righteousness; one seeking union with God for his soul's sake, the other how to be just with God for His righteousness' sake. Both are divine, but one has the calling and the entail and reversion of the world. The 51st Psalm is worth more for the future than the 23rd. If the centre of Christianity is still, in whatever form, justification by faith, then the former of the types contrasted is subordinate, or at least sequential. The Cross is the centre, source, and key of Christian ethic (which the Sermon on the Mount but illustrates). And its first Christian concern is a care that God should come by His own, that He should be righteous and holy, whatever become of man, or however He treat him—let God be true if all men are liars. Peace at any price is false Christianity, righteousness at any cost is true. The faith that justifies, that puts man morally right with God, is not simply a faith in free grace but in holy—a faith in its full righteousness, its royal right, and its final reign, a faith that the grace so free is also in the Cross just and triumphant on a scale universal and absolute. It is my faith that the God of Grace has secured in Christ His eternal righteousness, more even than that He has secured me. Such is the faith of the great saints. And it is not safe to differ with the great saints here. Their faith is, and must be, therefore, faith in an Atonement in which God's love first fully glorifies His holiness, one that does thus fulfil all righteousness, one that is, accordingly, the greatest moral Act of the Universe. It is an offering, primarily, not of pity but of sanctity, and neither by God to man nor by man to God but by God to God, the self-sacrifice of the perfectly holy Son to the perfect holiness of the Father.

The chief division between types of Christian belief turns on this—on the hegemony for the soul of conscience on a universal scale, on the primacy of righteousness, on the authority of the holy. But the sense of the holy (as beyond the merely reverend or august) is passing out of current religion; and with serious moral results. The former of the two types I named is anthropocentric religion. That is, its prime interest is man with God to help him (Ps. xxiii.); and it ends in subjective humanism, with God squeezed out. The other is theocentric, i.e. its prime interest is God, with man to worship and serve Him absolutely (Ps. li.). Its mysticism is objective and moral, and it ends in the Kingdom of God. The one is concerned with the freedom of the loving soul, which the other only finds in a prior and engrossing concern for the kingship of a holy God. The more subjective and humanist type must be second (however essential) in a historic religion whose first concern is with the guilt of the race, i.e. with the primacy of holiness. By itself it is individual or sectional. It is not catholic. It fails in range, amplitude, subtlety, flexibility, reality, and command. Like much sympathy it is liable to this-worldliness, and tends to subside to the homelier uses and needs. It represents the Local Government Board of the divine Kingdom. It is strong on personal conduct or kindness, but weak in moral range and insight. It is poor in its conception of righteousness; which rises little above individual integrity or purity within the minor social circles. Its uniting power for the world is not righteousness but fraternity, not conscience but kindness, not God but man. It finds its bond of human union in the one touch of nature, in men loving each other, instead of all being loved by God. It believes in conquering the position thus instead of being more than conquerors—being redeemed; in love as a work instead of love as a faith, in the love we practise instead of the love we trust. Consequently this type of mind has not the instinct which feels God to be on the field when He is most invisible. It finds Him in happy peace but not in crucial judgment, which is apt to break down its faith. Or, in respect of evil, it is preoccupied with the obvious anomalies of the day, but has not the *flair* for the grand iniquities, the world tragedies, for the deities and dominants of hell, for vast impersonal evil, for spiritual wickedness in high places. That means something graver than the shortcomings of bishops, the sins of the smart set, or the peccadilloes of Gaiety peers. The type of religion in view is shocked by the sins of camps but dull to the sins of thrones. It is horrified at the sins of cities, but it is not equally sensitive to the sins of earth's principalities and powers. Its idealism is millennial happiness rather than moral majesty. It lacks the sense of historic junctures, and public justice, and cosmic, imaginative righteousness. It has ethical interests but not moral insight. It is harder on Judas than on Caiaphas. It does not gauge sin on the demonic scale, nor an imperial righteousness. It views neither good nor evil in the historic dimensions of an actual Kingdom of

God among the nations, but chiefly on provincial or Socialist lines. Its very Church is 'a pneumatic democracy' without the aristocratic note. It is the Church catholic at the cost of the Church holy. In the State it knows nothing of a collective personality or a general will. It does not therefore realise national sin, though it uses the phrase, nor the need of a national righteousness to resist it.

National righteousness means much more than the sum of individual excellence; it means the righteousness which belongs to the nation as a moral unit, a moral personality, a moral subject on another plane than the individual, with a far wiser history, and a longer entail of responsibility. This, it should be realised, was the scale of the sin that slew Christ and doomed Israel. Israel did not fall by its individual and obvious immorality, by drunkenness, licentiousness, or worldliness among its common population, which was certainly better than Rome. It fell through a national choice made for God's honour by its eminently able and respectable leaders, to whom the people were sold and delivered. It was not the accumulation of the common sins of the common man that brought the doom, but State sin, high-placed sin, the solidary sin of the distinguished and cultured. It was sin on a scale imposing or dazzling, the illustrious perdition of the moral soul, the sin of people more religious than righteous, and hard on lapses but dull to judgment, the sin of devoted moral dunces, sin abetted by the Church of the land and its leaders, a sin common to its politicians or its popular leaders (who kept the commandments with Pharisaic severity), and to deserting disciples and betrayers. It was over the *city* that Christ wept. It was a national, a spiritual, an 'eternal' sin that slew Him, saturating the very religion of decent Israel, unredeemed by the purity, the wisdom, the kindness of a Hillel or a Gamaliel, and ending in a national doom, to none so surprising and crushing as to those who had done most to earn it. It was the sin that only religion can produce, the daintiest, may be, and comeliest sin, in many clothed with a piety that ruins moral judgment, takes the iron out of a man's blood, prevents it entering into the blood of his children, and finally turns pale the very blood of Christ. It was the sin of the most earnest and progressive of the people, people who believed in a righteousness of severe duty that let them crucify Heaven's Holy One and Just, the champions of the best religion and culture of the land. It was sin that found its apologists in all the professors and rabbinists of the day, the kind of elegant sin in which may be conjoined, at other junctures, religion and cruelty (as the Italian Republics showed). It was sin with a soft flesh, a fine hue, and a hard stone, the public sin that abjures humanity, repudiates humane morality, and yet sends people to the churches to pray for the success of that policy and the victory of such arms. It was the deep sin of Pharisaism adopted as a national programme, a moral vigour and rigour without moral insight or sympathy, ethical interest blind to evangelical principle, unlimited self-sacrifice for a damnable end of pious egoism—a kind of sin so spiritually discerned that none saw or felt it for what it was but its Victim. The sting and woe to Him in Gethsemane was the infatuation of His misguided nation, the godlessness of the good. What broke His heart was His tragic sense that its supreme Lover should be its fatal doom. There fell on Him the curse of the mixed blindness and wickedness of a whole humanity made concrete and historic in a nation. The evil power was pointed in a national crisis which held in it the salvation or the doom of a world. It was not a vague and dreamed humanity whose suffering lay on the Saviour's soul, nor was it the failure of an ideal programme of social ethic. His Cross was not chagrin at the collapse of a public programme and the rejection of a moral code. The wickedness of mankind was here concrete in a nation's supreme crime, as the righteousness of a loving God was gathered to a head in that nation's Victim. It was by a national crisis, brought to a sharp and bloody point, that the salvation of the world came. Is it wrong to say that so also it comes from time to time? It came by an issue of a nation's life or death on a matter of world moment and eternal right. The sin that slew Christ was sin in the grand style, sin worse than particular wars, Satanic sin, hard to discern, beyond the vision of a pedestrian ethic, and measurable only by the moral imagination. The ruin came by an 'eternal sin,' and not by a passing crime. The issue of the world-righteousness was decided in a historic form and in a national doom. That was (and is) the principle of its decision. The Christ of the atoning Cross loved men as they have never been loved, but He loved the world-righteousness of God's holy Love more, and in national terms. The

Kingdom of God was not in voluntary philanthropy alone, nor only in sympathetic atmosphere and kindly ways; but it was in a national obedience and insight. And it takes its course through the contact or collision of peoples who stir issues of a world-righteousness organic with that set up in the Cross.

There is a type of mind which is strong and sound on individual, domestic, and commercial morality, but weak on a righteousness conditioned by the whole course of history. It is full of a homely and hearty ethic rather than an imaginative and universal, an ethic of the primary colours, an ethic of honesty alone without the delicacy or distinction of honour. It has the moral mentality of youth rather than the tragic wisdom and prophetic strain of age. It is blind to the interactions of historic movement or national policy with the Kingdom of Satan, and it is dull to a world warfare on the scale and style of the Redeemer and His Redemption. It is not the state of its belief that is wrong so much as the scale of it, the note of it, which is apt to be provincial, sectarian, and in the end trivial. Its Christianity has its focus not really in the Cross, where the true universality of Christianity resides, but in the Sermon on the Mount, which is largely 'occasional.' It rallies not on the Cross which overcame the world by a new creation of the conscience, but on the precepts of the Teacher, which were there to guide and clarify the regenerate on whom the Cross had done its decisive work. It gathers not at the moral crisis and holy centre of the world, but round precious illustrations and fertile directions to the Church in a particular situation. It rests not on the righteousness the Cross set up for the world, but on a love esoteric to the Church. It reflects the too modern tendency to reduce public Christianity to a highly spiritualised ethic of patient sympathy between brethren (which men are not), together with an excessive concern for pain or life; and to ignore Christianity as the victory of love's eternal and universal righteousness, with its crucial imperative on the world even unto death. It does not see (in Goodwin's phrase) that in Christian love while the fond part is ours the real part is God's. It has learnt more from Tolstoi than from Paul. It expatiates in the sympathies of the Gospel, but it does not realise what Paul described as the power of the Gospel, and what he set mighty on the forehead of his greatest statement of it. He is not ashamed of the Gospel before great Rome because in it is revealed the righteousness of God, a righteousness greater than even Roman justice, and growing in an ascending scale of faith (Romans i. 17). That is the aspect of the Gospel that bears upon nations and States. The public form of love is righteousness. While the type of mind I have in view moves happily in the ideal beauties of a non-national Christian brotherhood, while it can even own God's judgment in public nemesis; yet it shrinks from the positive movement of God's holy Kingdom in peoples, and from the violence of the blood of the Cross (that founded the Kingdom) as the last and constant judgment of the world. It is a frame of mind which is largely a result of our modern concentration on the teaching of Christ to men of sensitive good will; to the neglect of His apocalyptic wrath, and of the Atonement in which He created the new ethic and the eternal. There he dealt a doom of saving blood once and for ever to the unrighteousness of mankind. But the piety I mean lives on the blessings of love, while a principle like justification by faith it finds only theological, and therefore but academic.

But the theology of a historic revelation is not a set of theses; it is a tissue of powers. However negligible it may seem within the few years of a man's life, it rules the moral course of generations, where alone it has room to turn round and come full circle. This pacific type of mind fails to see that, while the Love of God is the ruling spirit between the members of the ideal Church, the righteousness of God, striving even to blood, was, and is, the form of the issue between His Kingdom and the nations of the world, the spiritual man and the natural. Its religion lacks the virile, the dramatic, the tragic note, the note of historic conflict and moral victory therein. It does not realise that, as the settlement of that love's righteous issue on the Cross was the Church's one foundation, the ethic of that act, love's righteousness unto blood, is the Church's ruling principle. There God's holy love of the world, which did not spare His only Son violence and judgment, had its expression. It had its expression upward in the supreme moral act of Propitiation, and manward in the supreme moral act of Justification. But Justification, in the form of piety before us, is simply dismissed as archaic. It does not even undergo a moral re-interpretation to fit the age. It is not, as final righteousness, the moral focus and organising principle of the new life, the new morality, the New Humanity, on both the public and the private, on the eternal, scale. It is not what gives that New Humanity its moral quality. If it is understood at all, it is only as it concerns grace to me, mercy to me. It is not realised as a holy grace, which justifies itself to a cosmic and eternal righteousness in the same act as carries mercy to souls. It is but the justification of the sinner, it is not also the justification of God to His own moral self by an Atonement He makes in blood. The supreme interest of the New Testament is always the righteousness of the God of Love—the love that, however tender to the penitent, yet, as holy, takes its racial form and public effect in a sinful world by a moral way, by the Cross, by a public way of judgment-grace. But this current spirituality which we discuss is moral in its fruits rather than its essence, as if the root of its ethic were but in an arbitrary decree of God for order's sake, and not in a necessity of His inmost nature in the Cross revealed. And so it tends to overlook the righteousness at any price in the Cross, and the necessity of that war in heaven which reached its acme there. It is pre-occupied with Christianity as an ethical frame of souls or groups, and not with the one universal, cosmic, eternal Act of Holiness, which it takes a Church in its unity to realise, and which is missed by a divided Church. It does not read Christianity as the crisis of the moral universe, which vibrates in all history, rules its deep march, overrules its enterprise, and redeems and masters, even in blood, the crimes of heroes and not alone the vices of slaves. Among many devout groups, Christ, even when His history is taken seriously by such piety, is regarded too much as the legislator of the Kingdom (which was not His *métier* at all), yea, even as the saintly sage of the best natural ethic and man's inner light, instead of the Creator of the New Humanity in His regenerative Redemption and its covenant of blood. Such exponents seem rather a sect gathered round the founder of its programme than a Church round the Redeemer of the world-conscience. The ethic of their faith is in the realm of refined law rather than in the field of creative Gospel, and it tends to live more by detailed precept than by a costly Redemption. It makes more for the morals of a regulative code than of a reconstitutive Cross. It turns on a new ideal rather than on the new life, created by the moral victory of the Cross, and shaped by *its* moral principle, which is the supreme source and interpreter of every precept in the Gospels. The key-word of the New Testament is not love but holy love. It is more, it is its final triumph in that historic and national righteousness which is the first and loving concern of all holiness. It is not mere brotherliness, but the triumph of the righteousness of a holy Father on the scale of human brotherhood—on the scale of brotherhood as set up by the Cross in the new conscience of penitent love, and covering a New Humanity whose unity is holy, i.e. absolutely moral in the conscience. It is the righteousness of God and His Kingdom. First righteousness then peace, first the Kingdom then fraternity—that is the New Testament note and order. That is the core of any Christianity which is rooted in the new creation, and which is not merely the apotheosis of a spiritualised human nature. Faith in righteousness and its service of God, even to wounds and death, to judgment not accepted only but inflicted—that is the faith that is a nation's strength no less than a soul's, that exalts a nation, and makes it to be an agent of God's historic purpose and a satrapy of His Kingdom. Righteousness is the form divine love takes between men in nations, as it takes the form of affection between souls in a Church. It is the way love works in the Grace of the Cross, whose great problem was the world's unrighteousness, not man's indifference (for Israel was a zealot) but man's wickedness. Love in the culture of the Church has one aspect, in the judgments of the world another. But it is love still.

The ethic I criticise rests really, in many cases though not in all, on a spirituality more mystic than moral, and therefore less than evangelical. It is more subjective in *our* pity than objective in *God's* act. It also rests, like all mysticism which is more occupied with the soul than with the conscience, on the note of religious individualism which so fails us in public crises. Like Schleiermacher, it presses the God-consciousness of Christ's person on an orthodoxy in great need of it. But it stops where Schleiermacher did, with the mystic process and person of Christ, but of a Christ dispowered of the Cross and its poignant moral crisis for history. It lacks (I have said) historic sense, moral vision, or social control, being engrossed with those inner movements in man which are believed to reflect the inner *processes* of God rather than to respond to His great *Act.* This frame of mind is too much interested in the martyred Saint to think of His earthly death as the actual moral crisis even of Eternity. It is more occupied with a principle of sacrifice ascending through creation to Christ than with the sacrifice that descended on creation in Him to make the new and greater creation. The work of Christ was, in this view, no more than to bring in a spiritual type of righteousness, of which the law was indicative, but, through some jar, incapable. It condenses the light lighting every man, and it existed before Incarnation or Atonement. It becomes ours by an inner illumination, and is not created by Christ's historic deed, as if Christ had required men to believe in this light rather than in His Person and its crowning Act.

All this is part of the inability and indisposition of this type of religion to grasp the moral core and crisis of personality, to realise the mystery of iniquity, to lay hold of the cosmic moral tragedy as the focus of reality, to take the measure of historic righteousness in a waxing Kingdom, and the providential nationalism therein involved. It reflects (as I have said) the type of mind which is more apt for the intuition of ideas than for the sense of an actual situation. It basks in the ancient light of the world rather than thrills to its sting or throbs with its new life. It does not kindle to the world tragedy of the holy life amid the hopeless guilt. It does not gauge the grand juncture of the general conscience, nor realise the actual moral case of historic man before the righteousness of God. It does not duly feel *quanti ponderis sit peccatum.* Its nature is too idyllic to taste the moral bitterness of things. It fails to see that the absolute crisis of the race was in the moral crisis of the Cross. It underrates the Man of Sin, either by poverty or by generosity of nature. And it is by the same defect that it fails to appreciate now the world issue of life and death, the acme of divine judgment, presented by such a struggle as is going on in Europe between the prince of this world and the Lord its Righteousness. It has a certain moral aloofness, and a disconcerting impartiality as to affairs, which is apt to become an honest affectation, and a naïve superiority—too proud to fight. In belief it tends to be foreign to the idea of a Mediator in any other sense than a medium. Revelation, for it, is an enlightening avatar rather than a redeeming Act. It holds by the inner light in every man, whereof its historic Christ was the type rather than the Creator. It views this as the sole and sufficient seed of life, needing no Scripture nor Church—a view which is religious atomism. It does not know Grace except as the divine and multitudinous smile of benign forgiveness; whereas for the real taste of God's Grace we need to have known the taste of His wrath and the existence of His Law. It has not the sense nor need for a corporate Judgment, Atonement, and Regeneration, due to the whole righteousness of the universe, and creating a historic kingdom. It tends, with all idealists, to credit offhand the inner spirituality of man with final redemptive power—which is a very great leap. It would leave behind such chrysales as

Justification, from which it deems the soul has long emerged into flight; and it cherishes in consequence a non-ethical spirituality, or one, at least, whose ethic is a sequel rather than a constituent, and lies in its sympathetic fruits and not in its creative core and nature. It trusts an immediate light, an individual, and therefore an unhistoric, and therefore non-social, light, which has in it more piety than faith, and the bias to reflection rather than action, or, if to action, then to action private and non-corporate. It is denationalised, and it is de-churched; and it seems often to owe more to the occasional conferences of groups than to the common worship of the Church. Its Reconciliation is all of love and none of righteousness, being more generous to men than just to God, and resting on no Atonement as 2 Cor. v. 19 does on verse 21. Salvation was not effected by Christ in His moral and atoning victory, but only shown us in His fine teaching and winsome truth, His high precept and His gracious character. His death is not the agent but only the image, and symbol, and classic of the true Redemption, which is really within each man and His experience. The world was not in that death overcome for ever, all history morally mortgaged to a holy God, and all public righteousness impounded for His Kingdom, by the creation once for all of an eternal world-righteousness in and over the course of things. There is admitted, of course, a valuable connection between the Cross and history, but none necessary and creative; there is none such as those fathers of modern liberty, the Puritans, felt and embodied between that historic death, with its inner liberation of the soul, and the public liberation of a people in the world, to say nothing of the creation of a new people in a new world. The words and deeds of Christ are very precious and quickening to these groups, but they are only symbolic for souls, not effective for reality. They are more preceptual, exhibitory, or exemplary than sacramental. They show but do not convey, do not create. With such an idea of overcoming the world, the note of public righteousness, as something involved in the very nature of an atoning Reconciliation, is drowned in a haze of sympathetic love, or tangled, like the Pleiads, in a golden braid. This is a fine and fruitful phase in a time of order and peace; but in the present hour of death and day of judgment it is like shutting down the engines and expecting the crew to drive the ship, or trusting the compass to set the course. In the storm it has not a captain but only a cox. It calls on Mary, as it were, when Messiah is the need. It dwells on a city of dreaming spires, instead of a city whose salvation is as battlements and towers.

All my remarks in the last few pages do not apply to the Society of Friends, but many do—especially in connection with the real crisis of the whole moral world in the atoning cross of Christ. The treatment of this doctrine is the chief defect in Barclay's Apology (surely one of the finest books of its day and of many a day). But it is a defect so central ethically that, when a moral crisis should arise, of the first rank and on a world scale, transcending all philanthropy or mere veracity, it was bound to invite the disaster that the war has brought to the principles of the Friends and their cohesion.

I have said that the moral tone in such types

while it is proposed as superior, lacks the note both of the lofty and of the large, and especially the note of the deep, penetrative, judging, shattering, and re-creative Spirit, the note of an evangelical and revolutionary Gospel, and of a universal Church. It has the note of a young country with more civilisation than culture. It lacks action in the grand style. It has the note of moral sectarianism, of a culture self-disinherited of the past and secluded from the collective continuity and influence both of Church and State. Or, if it is not secluded, then it is influenced but negatively, by way of antagonism instead of obligation. It renounces the great moral legacy of our providential place in a historic train and spiritual tradition of the race which has done more to make every citizen than he can do to make himself. It ceases to be an actual citizen through a notion of citizenship in an abstract Kingdom of God. It is in its country but not of it. Now the sects have been of the greatest value to the Church, and such sectional ethic as I describe has been, in the case of the Quakers, and in issues only civil or social, of unspeakable worth to society. And, if Christianity were but earnest pity, noble philanthropy, shrewd veracity, and thoughtful fraternity, it would be of supreme worth. But it is quite inadequate to the great judgment days when the world is in a convulsion of warring nations, powers, and principles, days which shudder with a prelude of the last trump, when the prince of this world is challenged in his anarchic power and reign. Here the spirit of the ethical sect is unequal to the vast situation; and it must rise and regain the catholic note of a moral

Church with national import when its good work is done. If it do not, it sinks into a mere provincialism of the conscience, which it deludes itself in thinking to be the true but hidden Kingdom of God. So a worthy antagonism to the State's Erastian claim on the Church may drop to an ignoble antagonism to all claim by the Christian State on the Christian duty and sacrifice of its members; who, if they refuse, nursing a prickly conscience and an atomic liberty now far on its way to dissolve society, cease to be members of the State and become its parasites. They live in facilities secured by others who do not shrink from the sacrifices which they refuse to the nation calling in her last stress. 'But every member of a group, in so far as it is a moral association, should be unwilling to benefit by any act of his representatives which he would be ashamed to do for himself.'[1] And Mazzini says, 'Your country is the sign of the mission God has given you to fulfil towards humanity.' The citizens of a great old nation, if they believe at all that God has been guiding and using it for His Kingdom, should recognise its great, rare, moral calls as their bounden duty and service, voluntary but not chosen in self-will, rather laid on them from God in the way of His historic Providence with us. God does not care for one nation above another, but a nation is as needful as a home is for His Kingdom, and for our moral and spiritual growth therein. Surely a religion has sunk as a moral religion which encourages us to live chiefly on the sacrifice of others; or which, should it own sacrifice, owns it only in some self-selected form, withdrawing us from the claim of humanity in the

[1] Delisle Burns, *Political Ideals*, p. 203.

concrete form, a historic crisis that is no mere tussle of nations but a crisis in the history and fate of the race. For a nation to repudiate national morality, as Germany has done in word and deed, is to take up arms against the Kingdom of God; it is to organise civilisation in the service of the Kingdom of Evil; it is to sin the sin against mankind which God has given mankind the office to arrest and to judge if there be international duty at all. It is to transpose a national war into the awful key of the Lord's controversy with the world; it lifts a campaign to this scale. But there are several types of religion, and even of Christianity, where sacrifice escapes from both the control and the benediction of duty, and an inward light becomes a subtle form of spiritual self-will—by which sin fell the angels. It is not a question of personal courage (which many freely, if perversely, show in their defiance of public obloquy) but of a type of religion which doth the human spirit cool, reduces an apostle to a humanitarian, takes the red from the blood of Christ, and turns the courage of faith to be but the patience of the saint.

There is but one situation in which a servant of God may discard his nation and leave it to the heathen powers without. Jeremiah took that course, and Jesus. It was because they were convinced that the moral state of the people was hopeless for the historic purpose of God with it. And, if we became sure of the same thing about Britain, that might be our only Christian course. Those who take that course to-day should be clear in their minds that such is the state of the country. But they should also be sure that theirs are minds with the qualities of moral insight and judgment that qualify for such a sentence on our complex present, and our long and (though stained) not quite ignoble past.

The point of the whole is that a type of religion, part humanist, part mystic, and all too unhistoric, has engaged the interest of large numbers of people, especially among the young, and such as are by nature as yet more in love with man than with righteousness, and who resent wrong more than they measure sin. To their prompt, subjective, and unschooled sympathies a moral matter like justification by faith is ancient and otiose. The source of this temper is partly reaction from theology, as they have heard of it. And, indeed, if justification by faith were but a theological theme, instead of the vital religion of the Christian man (to whom conscience is even more than heart, and the Cross a salvation as well as an appeal), one could not wonder, nor criticise. But, in one form or another, justification, with its moral verve, is the very central point of an ethical Christianity, and of its Kingdom's righteousness subduing the world. It is not an idea to be absorbed, but among the chief of those energies that fashion and command us. It is not a thesis but a great power. It concerns the Grace of God as righteous, holy Grace, requiring the Cross. And the type of religion that ousts it from real concern to make room for pious impression or imaginative mystic produces an ethic too indifferent to the righteousness of God's Kingdom to rule men, and too human to meet human need. This righteousness of God was the first charge on Christ's love in His Cross. And a religion on which it is not also the first charge, however attractive that religion may be, is too limited ethically to be equal to a moral world crisis of the first magnitude like to-day's. It moves also at last, as in the recent case of a prominent preacher of this type, to seek the objective it uneasily lacks in a sacramental system instead of a positive Gospel. It becomes therefore pacific and aloof (with all its kindly light) when the more robust and evangelical conscience goes to the Lord's help against the mighty. Justification is an experience and not a thesis, an experience of the conscience too, and not merely of the emotions. With its faith of the conscience (and of the race's conscience) giving the moral lead to charity, it affects the whole quality of Christianity, especially in its relation to society and to historic junctures. It is not at last a question of *love* between men over against *righteousness* between men, but of the love and righteousness between holy God and evil man, between love as communion where it meets love and love as saving judgment where it does not. It is the difference between a mystic communion of love and a righteous kingdom of love. It is a question of the application and exercise of God's love ; which exercise is one thing within a Church of the regenerate, and another thing as righteous discipline and judgment-grace towards a yet unregenerate world. The salvation of God is, to those who are but in a relation of law, righteousness ; but to those who are joined in Gospel it is love. In the one it is law, judgment, war ; to the others joy and peace in the

Holy Ghost. But always love and always holy at any cost to life or limb.

First righteousness, then peace. And, if righteousness be no mere matter of a local conflict between quarrelling nations, but of an Armageddon in the Lord's controversy with the world, then even war can be a call to the service of God's Kingdom.

And we may see how that which seems but a theological issue, like justification by faith, creates a certain type of religion, which is an asset of prime value in a practical national issue of the last moment for God's Kingdom. We may see how closely it is bound up, by its stress on universal righteousness, with national existence; and how the type which lacks it lacks also the due sense of a nation's dignity in its moral vocation, which is service to the Kingdom of God, resisting if need be even to blood.

We are now more than soldiers. We are of the international police. We are there neither for conquest nor merely for self-defence, but for the world order, liberty, justice, and humanity for which Christ died. Or did He not? With Mazzini we would rescue the sons of men from the bastards of mankind. We are set for a world-righteousness. And that is the cause for which the Father spared not His only Son, even to the shedding of blood. If righteousness be the public form of love, may we not, in the awful conflict and bitter agony, rise to say that we so love the world as to give our beloved sons for it and for its future. 'Therefore will I give men for thee and people for thy life.'

CHAPTER VIII

CHRISTIAN ETHIC LAY AND HISTORIC

SEVERAL references in the course of discussing the historic and practical issues in this great crisis may have prepared us for certain questions which lie behind them all. Matters of particular ethic are subordinate to such a question as that of the source and standard of all ethic; for of course our judgment on particular cases will depend entirely on the standard of principle with which we approach them. This inquiry as to ultimates may not seem to all to be called for; and indeed it is not every man's affair. It is one of those matters that are settled by a comparatively few, whose results filter down in course into the general mind. To an extent we all act as laymen in a Church of authoritatives.

From what has been said it may be clear that in the writer's view there is no final ethic but a Christian and a theological. The greatest conscience of all the world must in His greatest Act be the source of all morals if He is the source of Eternal Life. I am well aware how much prejudice the word theological may raise, and especially even in some whose objection is taken in the interest of ethic. For they say that theology not only takes away interest that ought to be given to ethic, but that the ethic in theology is of an inferior, and even mischievous, kind. Now this is a frame of mind not hard to understand, as theology has too often been pursued and pressed. It has been treated as if it were but theosophy, a branch of a hidden wisdom, instead of the moral mind in God's public word to man; as if it were a secluded metaphysic of the divine instead of the marrow of His saving message to the conscience of the race; as if it were the hobby of certain Christians whose religion developed intellectual tastes, a scheme of ideas which had no more bearing on affairs than mythology on appendicitis, a collection of truths which have about as much relation to progress as a museum of walking-sticks, a series of notions which at best are but truths only, and the appanage of pious thinkers who know little of history and less of the world. Whereas in ethic, they say, we want powers. It is for a practical purpose that we are here. It is for action that we are made, and our chief intellectual concern is with the principles that move or guide action on the personal, and especially on the historic, scale. In reply to such wholesome critics it must be owned that the source of theology is action and not thought. It is history. It is a historic Act with a quality, meaning and effect which, whatever else it is, is moral at the productive and creative centre. The Cross of Christ is the crisis of the eternal and immutable morality. But it has been treated as a means of escape if we neglect so great a salvation as conscience brings.

Again, there are some (preachers mostly) who feel an aversion to theology without being devotees of ethic, whose interest is not so much moral as sympathetic, who certainly feel that we must have more than bare truths, but who, being unable to command power, take refuge in a halfway house called impression. Such truth as they have does not yield power, but it can be made to contribute to impression. And they are tempted to think that weekly impression may do the work of some great and perennial principle which is the source of a continual regeneration. That is hardly possible when we deal radically with will and conscience; for, while impression may be moral in its nature, regeneration must be. The one affects us, the other changes us. The one may stir manhood, the other makes a new man of it. The one is food, the other is vitality. The one is a tonic, the other is power. And the Christian doctrines, if they are living at all and not dried specimens, wield something more than mere stimulus; they are vital powers because they go beneath the sympathies to the fountains of life in will and conscience. There is at times a certain feud (which can even be rude) between the preacher and the professor. The former does not see that impressionism will not meet the moral problem of Christianity without regeneration (though he does feel the drain it makes on himself, and often succumbs to it); he stirs interest more than he conveys power. While the latter has often failed to realise that regeneration is not a theme, nor a magic, mystic, merely individual thing, but that it is the deep action of Christ in history and on history, and not on the Church alone. For the regenerate Church is the inchoate stage of the New Humanity and of the Great History that is to be.

In so far as theology is pious speculation or intellectual hobby it has no more claim on the general attention than theosophy or any other hobby of an academic kind. And it has nothing much to do with the soul and its salvation as a conscience. But Christian theology is in no such case. Its doctrines are not mere theses but forces, and its cohesion is not mere system but the mentality of Eternal Life. It arose out of history, out of the union of a historic revelation with a historic situation. History is its milieu. Its form has been much shaped by history, and it has still much to do in the way of shaping it. It aims, indeed, at the capture of history. The object of God's will and purpose of love is mankind as one, mankind as an organism, mankind in its totality—in its moral totality round the redeeming conscience of Christ and His Reconciliation. And those doctrines of Redemption are the sinews of that moral and historic organism. They are the thews of Christ's body politic. They are not the peculium of groups. For the Bible teaches no eternal election of a particular section of individuals. The great doctrines are not mere dogmas; they are moral powers; they are historic powers. And by that is meant not only that they have played a great part (if often an unhappy one) in history, but that they embody the moral principles on which society must live, and history must run more and more if it is moral, and if it is moving for a Kingdom of God at all. The righteousness swift and complete in the Cross is the same righteousness which is slowly making the kingdoms of the natural world into the righteous Kingdoms of a holy God. All history in its deep long meaning, in its slow substantial meaning, is Christ coming into His own. It is the self-exposition, the self-effectuation, of the Redeemer. The great Christian doctrines are the moral tracks of His Kingdom. They are the nervous system of the whole body and movement of history as it is bespoken for Christ. They are not academic to Christianity nor otiose to the world, but they are morally organic to the history of humanity as the New Humanity which Christianity intends. They are not for seminaries but for pulpits and parliaments—not indeed as creeds, but as directives and dominants. The mind which is not critical only but also sympathetic, nor is theologically illiterate but has been caught at the formative age and trained on the classics in this kind, will, I trust, grasp what I mean, whether it go all the way with me or not. The Christian doctrines cover principles and forces which, working in all history, guide it to the Kingdom of God. They are much more than religious ideas in precipitate. They are moral, spiritual, creative powers. A philosophy of history traces the movement of ideas of which the chief actors were quite unconscious, and which only a later age can discern. But that is not the part played by the great Christian doctrines, which rather created and moulded great men both in the Church and in the world. For they were the conscious possession, experience, and principle of these great figures, whether we take for our instance a Cromwell, or a Hildebrand, or a Bernard. Christianity is a historic religion not only as appearing in history, but as congenial to it, taking command of it, and controlling its development with a destiny and bias forgone and imperative. Its central doctrines do but form the source or the condensation of those moral powers, so urgent and so final, to which we look for the conversion of human history from a welter of egoist dragons tearing each other in slime to all that arrests the moral imagination as the Kingdom of God.

These doctrines are the idioms of the largest living consciousness of the Church. They are both expressions and agents of an imaginative moral realism which is as full of human passion as of divine power. The blood of Christ is the sap of humanity. The moral catholicism of the New Humanity is in the atoning Cross of Christ, which is the crisis of man's moral tragedy, at once the focus of the first creation and the source of the new. History is the long and struggling fulfilment of Christianity, which is its prophecy, and not only its prophecy but its producer. The love of God is more mighty than all progress; and the judgment of God in the Cross of Christ is a thing more terrible than any wars; it is the ruling principle for interpreting all the other and inferior judgments in history, however great. It is a misfortune that its true moral majesty should have been claimed and belittled by the ethic of the greybloods, who are more shocked with the patent sins of the streets and tribunals than by the deadlier sins of cabinets, which make the arbitrament of war. I read once of the pity due to a virtuous man embarrassed by the necessity of doing something important.

I venture therefore to follow up what I have said by a discussion which is theological in the great sense I have described, but which may be passed over by any who wish to confine their attention to that range of ethical interests which they may consider the layman's province.

We are being carried by the line of thought in our preceding chapters into the inmost questions as to the source and genius of Christianity.

It seems a hard saying, but one of the banes of modern religion is its Idealism. And for Germany the one has ruined the other. It can be as fatal as Materialism, which it can idealise.

The Bible knows nothing of idealised man, but of man redeemed and reborn. It founds on justification, and it insists on repentance from all. And repentance is the soundest destroyer of our illusion. God is not the supreme Idealist. He is our Redeemer. He is under no illusions about man, since He has to do everything for him.

No doubt in a country such as Germany, or France, or England was in the early nineteenth century, Idealism was a precious gospel. In the face of a Materialism both theoretical and practical it was much to the good both of morals and imagination. When the soul cleaves to the dust anything is welcome that gives it wings—whether in the region of religion, art, philosophy, literature, worship. All such things are visitations from the High God. But, in His Church at least, the Eternal is no mere visitant. And it is not His visitation that we need most but His indwelling power. We cannot live on the wing. We must have renewals always sure. We must have footing, moral strength, the power, the majesty, and therewith the eternal patience, of God. In this respect Idealism needs to be saved from itself. It needs power, and power beyond inspirations that come and go. Above all things, above even the power of God periodically renewed, we need a perennial spring, a faith which is a new life. We need faith as power to trust ourselves and our world to His power. And not for what that power may do but for what it has done; and we need this faith for life, in the way of a new birth and a new life for mankind. We must trust Him for a Kingdom coming because come—sure, final, and eternal. That is faith. It is no mere expression of moral ardour, of the enthusiasm of the conscience as an enthusiasm of humanity might be felt. Greater that the doctrine of moral personality, its conscience, and its culture, is that of a secure Redemption, by which alone the moral personality comes to its own at last, by a regeneration growing up it knows not how. Faith is trust in what God has done in this way for good and all, trust in the great decisive thing not as one day to be done but as done once for all. It is trust in a fundamental moral realism. It is trust in a Kingdom come, and working out mightily through everything. If our chief interest be but in the ideal future there is always some uncertainty. Has the ideal its own guarantee? Can it give itself effect, bring itself to pass, and not only evolve but redeem? What if an accident happened to the idea on its course? How can we be perfectly sure that it will arrive? How can faith in final good be absolute if all things are but on their way to the great goal, on their tentative way

—if they are only working towards some Great Event and not working it out, if our last faith do not trust it as already done and secure in all but its actual effect with human wills? Faith is in its nature absolute and final; it is not probablist; it does mean such certainty and trust of a *fait accompli* in God. Whereas Idealism means but the fine sense that it should be, and the highest hope that it will be, done; and a fine faith need not be a final. The Christian morality, the righteousness which is of faith, is not simply an *ought* but an *is* which involves an ought. It is not a noble *ought* but a glorious *is*, to eyes unsealed. It ought to be on earth because it already is in the heaven within earth. But to a mere ideal anything may happen.

I have been speaking of the movement, philosophical and imaginative, known as Idealism. But it would be a rash thing to say that all idealism is of this kind, or is to the good. For we are faced in Germany with the extinction of the old Idealism (which had become its chief religion) and the growth of an idealism which is but materialism glorified to a megalomania, a combined worship of Mammon, Mars, and Mercury (thief and liar), a compound of militarism, commercialism, and a nationalism based on these, rooted in force, and reckless of morals. That is an idealism divorced both from thought and from faith—the idealism of the man of sin. But the Germans only do very thoroughly what others are moved to do with less audacity. They go on to do what we did at a stage, but what, under Christian influence, we have been striving to atone for by such a practical repentance as our treatment of India, and South Africa, and the smaller nationalities. There is much to repent of and to renounce in the way we came by both India and the Cape. And if our moral frame is not changed or changing there is more than a little truth in the charges of hypocrisy that our enemy adds to his shells.

Even under the guise of peace, and in home affairs, practical idealism can be very heady stuff. Intoxicating many who are unaccustomed to the handling of ideas, it may bring with it a fatal impatience, and carry more sail than ballast. We are led by it to feel as if everything depended on us to realise the idea; and we become eager, and even nervous, to reach it before some accident cross its path, before our strength fail, or the victims die. Among the working classes, for instance, there never was a time of so much idealism as distinct from faith, nor of so much danger for us all because of their impatience for their ideal. True, it is a class idealism, and in so far an egoist idealism, and therefore it is the less pure. But that might not be so fatal apart from its impatience for some grand *coup* like a general strike, to end the crisis by force, and wreck society by aggressive war within. And this is but one instance of what I mean. The women went in the same way. But the habit and principle of faith destroys this fatal haste in destroying uncertainty. Faith knows that the great thing for the race's history, for the New Humanity, is substantially done and cannot be shaken or lost. We have but to wait on the opportunities of getting it into the actual course of history, and the daily experience of souls. The destiny of mankind is as sure as God and the soul. God has secured that. We are not dependent on the course of events for a belief in God, or His salvation, or our destiny. The great transaction is done. And if the path of its realisation among men be through desert, hill, sea, or earthquake which casts the hills into the sea, that does not destroy the soul's rest, patience, or power, its work, sacrifice, or worship. Faith is fixed on God's eternal saving Act for history, sure beyond the reach of any catastrophe that history may show.

The idealist movement has had a very great effect on the modern type of religion, in which there are few things more conspicuous than the unrest, impatience, and impotence of which I have spoken. And the reason is, as I say, that what it has gained in idealism it has lost in positive faith. But it is not idealism, it is faith that pleases God, works with Him, brings His Kingdom, draws on His Almighty Power, and is stayed on His victorious finality. The reason why I suggested that one of the banes of modern religion is its idealism may now appear. It has replaced historic and apostolic faith by imaginative hope, and by dropping the principle of an actual Justification in the dream of an ideal justice it has lost in moral power what it has gained in sympathetic interest. It has lost ethically and gained æsthetically. And what the soul of the world most needs is neither interest, nor even sympathy, nor charm. It is power. It is moral power. And that is what positive Christian faith gives—power to see God's practical way, power to trust it, power to take it, power to pursue it, and power to secure it. If it do not give that it is better gone. It prevents prayer for something that will give us the power. Let it go, and let us give ourselves to the new quest. For many indeed it has gone. We are living in a dense, almost stifling, atmosphere of precepts, impressions, ideals, and sympathies; and we are not in tonic contact with the powers and realities whose principles prescribe methods. We have been brandishing liberty when we should have been exercising service. We are more interested in being free than in being right, more concerned about being free with God's help than about being obedient to His Grace. (For freedom, you see, is humane and important, but Grace is only theological and negligible.) Our freedom we do not feel that we owe entirely to His Redemption. His very love has slackened our passion for His righteousness; or it has shrunk our notion of His righteousness to fraternal behaviour or mere fair play. The Church He redeemed with His blood falls into kindly groups of mystics, or camps of free lances. We become good and inept, devout and trivial. We form coteries and lose the nation. And we only manœuvre, because we are powerless to mobilise. What we need is power from on high, to make us wonder, and worship, and forget ourselves after a godly sort; what we keep craving is attention from the Purveyor of our salvation.

Were this impotence the general note of the Church its days would be measured and its creed doomed, but for some great new departure and creation of the Spirit. And some devout souls are already waiting and looking for that new departure, as if, through the calamities of the time, the Spirit would break with a mystic light and vision whose effect would be to scrap the old creeds and provide a new revelation. But this would really mean a new religion. And the Church can never admit a new religion. It stands there in trust of the final revelation, and therefore of the final religion. And whatever new thing awaits us must be a fresh ray from the old faith, and a fresh shoot from the old creed. That creed is much pollarded, and even hacked; but its substance remains when it is lopped —the holy seed is the substance thereof.

I have not forgotten my brief for an ethic both evangelical and national. What I have been saying is illustrated by the state of Christian ethic revealed by the present crisis, which is testing and sifting so much else. Many who wish to obey Christ in such a juncture are at sea as to what His will is; and largely because they have never taken any serious pains to ask such questions when their mental foundations were being laid, nor to submit to be taught in quarters where real teaching is to be found. For most, at their early stage at least, the liberty to choose their teacher is the chief responsibility and the best freedom they have, and it is the liberty most full of result. But so many are more eager to get out their raw views than to wait upon the wise. They want to be themselves more than to be right. They are more concerned to develop their own individuality than to let the truth do it for them. But a chief part of Christ's will is that we should go to school in the proper quarters as to what His will is. Yet there is nothing we dislike and distrust so much. We court the tickler and dread the teacher. Or we will not let the teacher speak for anxiety to get our own crudities out. That, it is claimed, is democratic freedom. We will take joyfully the spoiling of our goods, and especially of our neighbour's, rather than give up our self-will and our self-confidence in picking up Christ's will out of a meagre experience, or the face value of Scripture. We will trust Him with our soul—if He will lay it up in lavender, and do not ask us to give up our amateur constructions of His will for our conduct, if He do not expect us to take as much pains, or seek as much help, in learning to understand Him, as in making money, asserting our conscience, or producing pulpit effect. But He certainly does ask these surrenders for proficiency of soul, for proficiency of the moral soul. Only our care for that is lost in the kinder efficiencies and experiences—till at last the flood comes upon our spiritual eating and drinking, our lyrical pieties and our ethical societies, and we are caught unready for a real moral drain upon us. We have been too much with the religious troubadours and too little with the knights of the *Holy* Cross. The junctures that call for soul proficiency are fewer than the genial occasions, but they are much more crucial and creative.

If such a moral amateur as I have described is asked what the source of Christian ethic is, Christ straightway stands before him as the idealist legislator; and his readiest answer is that it is the precepts, or at most the teaching, of Christ, and particularly the Sermon on the Mount. One reason for his answer is that he is a plain person (he says) and needs plain directions; and when he is taken away from the words of Christ he is cast on theology, for which he has no more use than Cobden had for Thucydides. It would be extraordinary—the way instructed people, even learned clergymen with the epistles before them, seem yet to lack the idea of any source of Christian ethic or conduct but the teaching or example of Jesus—were that notion of theirs not but a part of the general disposition of their time to go round the Cross, and to dislodge it from the creative centre of the whole regenerate soul. It is not Christ that is now denied but His Cross. In the case of the clergy, it may be a sign of the traditional inability of a patristic culture to give the Cross its central and genetic place, the place which was recovered for it from the New Testament only after a clerical millennium and more. So original and profound was its essential note that it lay hidden all that time, though not inert. This tendency has produced, under the guise of escaping from theological subtleties, a certain spiritual hebetude, a blunting of the religious nerve and verve, which makes such people impatient when they are called on for religious effort that does not allow of a committee on it, or for a really ethical type of religion, or one that draws upon some study, and not merely a glimpse, of the Christian reality. In religious reviews, for instance, which propose to interpret the Church's belief, I have been much struck with the frequent contrast in an article between the sweep of the title and the shrinkage of the text; as if the title were a borrowed phrase and the treatment original dilution; as if the writer read more than he studied, and was sprinkled with his subject rather than immersed in it. The article has a large programme on its front but the body of it is a body of humiliation. Its effect is to bring down the great issue to a level of obvious truth, vague edification, and exasperating piety, such as a few hard-working clergy could listen to while they digested a milk lunch, and before they rushed off to a round of parish trivialities.

But apart from the amateur's generosity with his small change, the Christian conscience and thoroughness have to contend with a dominant type of religion whose tendency is to becloud the ethical core of Christianity in a mystic or a genial haze. The white passions, or the grey, bedim the red and their reality. The blood of Christ is made of no effect. Love is stripped of wrath. Death is detached from judgment. The worm dies and the fire is quenched. God ceases to be a consuming fire, and only flickers on the family hearth, the fraternal group, or the spiritual circle. He does not rule among the nations, He only works in the societies. He is held to be more near in unction than in conscience, and in the private conscience more active than in the public. Take any group at random of the members of the Church below middle age. Take especially the young end. Question them. Ask if they can remember ever having heard a sermon or a lesson upon the anger of God, or upon the terrible things in righteousness which answer our need of salvation or our hunger for love. Their persuasion, such as it is, did not come from men who knew the terror of the Lord but only a winsome Jesus. Allusions there may have been by their teachers, or phrases reminiscent of an age when the wrath of the Lamb was a reality; but never anything to indicate that such judgment is an element as vital to a holy God as they hold His pity is to a God of love. One may tell you that he used to hear that God loved the sinner while hating the sin—which is a meaningless phrase and a psychological anomaly. It separates sin from a sinning personality, and reduces it therefore to a mere abstraction, incapable of rousing the wrath of a real God. Such talk but swells the froth on the water of life. Not one will tell you of any help given to conceive of God (with Paul, for instance, in Romans xi. 28) as at once loving and hating the same personality in the Gospel, in the very purpose and act of redeeming it. That is to say, a whole hemisphere of the nature of God, all the holiness of His love, was practically left out of their religious training. Think what that means, repeated at many centres and spread over a whole generation. These catechumens were reared to worship but a demigod. They knew but a kind God over against a hard world—as if God were all kindness and the world all hardness; and neither is true. As if the Christian revelation was God's love, instead of the sure and final power of God's love to overcome everything, and of God's holiness to establish itself everywhere. The ethical, the holy, element in God's love, that which gives it its dominion, its stability, its eternity, was practically left out of their religion. The element of righteousness and judgment wherewith He rules among the nations was not there. They know nothing of ethic in the great vein. And as a consequence our youth was sent out of our Churches with no conscience *in* its religion. But it had a general, just, and clean notion of conscience in the ordinary moralities and chivalries, which it tacked *on to* the religion. The religion in itself was of a kind more excellent in style than moral in nature. It was too exclusively sympathetic to feel anything like command in a complex moral situation such as the modern world presents. It was apt to lack the historic scale, the national note, the moral genius, the prophetic apostolicity. In the result, when great public questions challenge the Christian conscience, this type has a conscience only on an individual or domestic scale—on a claustral scale at the utmost. It is unequipped for the moral reading of such huge forces as now are loose. It cannot even understand or measure them. It can stand up to imps but not to Satan. The gentle maxims of a sequestered place may be brought out to settle a crisis of our whole earth. The communities which live on such religion must lose weight with a public reared in business or other schools which have grit and gumption but still need a moral guidance that it is the duty of a practical, a historic, and an ethical religion to provide. A Christ and a Cross which have been so de-ethicised as to become but the one a prophet, the other an object-lesson, of God's love cannot maintain moral manhood. A cross so de-ethicised that the love in it has lost the whole idea of expiation for sin and judgment upon it is a Cross demoralised. And it can be the source neither of ethic nor conscience, as the focus of moral redemption must be.

CHAPTER IX

CHRISTIAN ETHIC HISTORIC AND NATIONAL

The matter of Christian ethic is often more difficult than that of Christian theology, from which so many think to find in ethic an escape. And this is shown by the varieties of uncertainty that come to light in connection with the very first step. What is the source of Christian ethic ? Is it historic revelation or inner light ? Is it national or just humane ?

If we try to answer in a radical way we must surely recognise that its source can only be the same as the source of the soul's Christian life. The supreme conscience of the world, in His supreme Act, must be the source of Christian morals if He is the source of Christian life. The rule of living must lie in the principle of life. Yet this is not what everybody would own. A crude notion is that our soul receives its new life (when a new life is really meant, and not merely an old life refurbished) from one source, say from the Cross of Christ, or from sacraments, and that then, in due course, its ethic as Christian is supplied to it from another source. The injunctions of the Church, or the teaching of Christ, or the precepts of the non-theological parts of the epistles are dropped into the vague new good will.

The matter of the ethic is preceptual, the Cross but provides the sanction or the impulse to do it. This unhappy idea is the result of the de-ethicising of the interior of the Cross consequent on sacramental theories on the one side, and of starved evangelical ideas on the other. The function of the Gospel in the former view is an infusion of new vitality (which need not be moral but finely physical); in the other it is a theological arrangement, which is not so much forgiveness (and therefore not moral) but only a juristic condition preliminary to forgiveness. As a result, forgiveness is not realised to be the supreme moral act of the Holy Love, but is regarded as a merciful provision for our escape from a moral region which has become too inclement or oppressive for our spiritual health. As the preacher on Heb. ii. 3 put it, while his first head was the greatness of the salvation, his second contained directions how to escape if we neglected it.

So far, however, is the Cross from being but incidentally and indirectly ethical that, as the greatest moral Act of Time or Eternity, it is the greatest Act of a holy God's creation, and the very source and norm of all ethic universal and eternal. (For it is only in the moral region, the region of our miraculous freedom of will, that we can form any conception of what creation is.) The thing the Cross had to do was to destroy a world sin by the supreme moral Act of the universe. And the destruction of sin could only take place by righteousness on a like scale. But this, if we grasp the inveteracy of sin, means a regeneration. It means a resurrection of the conscience from the dead, or at least from a paralysis only too perceptive for our peace. The Cross is therefore the most creative thing we know—the creator of the Kingdom of God and the New Humanity. The Act that ends sin is something more than erasure therefore. It has eternal moral quality and power, which is not sequential merely but intrinsic to it. It was a moral transaction. It is the centre, spring, and principle of a universal ethic, both as the highest Act of a holy God from heaven, and as the power of social righteousness on earth. The Cross founds in history the righteousness of the Kingdom of God and the New Humanity.

Great and moving indeed is the power of love. Nothing is so effective and impressive *while it lasts*. It is love, love, love that makes the world go round. But *sub specie eternitatis* what is there in it to guarantee that it will last, will survive, will round off the world, and conquer all the adverse possibilities of the unknown? Often enough it does not outlive the mutations of Time. Fine, also, and mighty is the power of man's loyalty, whether to his brother or to his chief. But what is there in loyalty between men to warrant our making it a religion absolute and for ever? Is it given to loyalty to have life in itself? The greatest thing in the world is not love, as the phrase would be understood by most who welcome it. It is something that can stay and comfort when every object of affection on earth is swept away. The greatest thing in the world is something out of it. It is *holy* love alone that has the promise and potency of an indomitable life. It is love inseparable from absolute righteousness with its moral necessity to establish itself everywhere, and its moral power in the Cross to do it. It is love with righteousness not as its happy sequel but as its intrinsic nature and purposed object. Great is love to heal a heart or to break it. And great is loyalty, which may pass even the love of woman. But greatest of all is the Gospel of holy love, of love's absolute, and self-sufficing, and ubiquitous righteousness, which is the guarantee of its victory and eternity. This is the catholicism of eternity—what unites Protestant righteousness with Catholic love. The triumph, the universality, the eternity of love is due only to its essential feature of holiness, so neglected by all the poets of passion and the hierophants of the great human heart.

And where do we find this holy love? For there is the source of Christian ethic; the source of the new life must be also its norm. We find it neither in the affections nor the intuitions of the individual heart, but in Christ. And it is not in Christ's conviction and teaching, nor in His example, but in His great creative and crucial Act behind all His teaching and beneficence. It is in the Cross, where is the one all-comprehensive gift of a holy God, and the one constant source and principle of the new life. It is in the Cross of our regeneration, a Cross at once historic and holy. By its atoning holiness it has in it the absolute principle of all morality, by its connection with Israel the principle of national morality, by its solidarity with history the principle of morality universal and public. By its work on the soul it is mystic, by its work in society moral. It makes the mystical union with Christ moral, and the moral union mystic. It thus unites soul and conscience, faith and life, piety and publicity. By its universalism it makes our new life organic with the ultimate moral movement in history, and its principle concrete with the deep course of public things. The Cross as the public satisfaction and revelation of God's *holiness* is the source and principle of Christian *ethic*, private and social. *There* is both the impulse and the law of Christian conduct. There we have moral utterance large enough for the society or nation in which the individual has his being. Love (as the holy and atoning Cross creates love), and do as you like. That is Christian ethic. It will bring us out at the long last at the Sermon on the Mount, if we do not begin and end there.

In the teaching of Christ we have applications and illustrations of this principle, but the principle itself in its power came to us by nothing so pinched as legislation or precept, but by action. It came by the action of a person, and of a providential and public person that at once condensed a nation into itself and judged it; by regenerative action, on that public and national scale, upon the race. It came by a new birth which is the entrance of man, through nationality and its subsumption, on a new moral world. It is the Cross that interprets the Sermon not the Sermon the Cross. We come to the Sermon with the Cross, not to the Cross with the Sermon. Even if the Sermon is to be taken for its principle rather than its precept, that principle is given us where the whole Christ is—in the Cross, the atoning, redeeming, regenerating Cross. In the teaching *totus Christus adest; sed non totum quod in eo est;* that was not put forth till the Cross. The instruction in the Sermon was not regenerative (no instruction, no precept, is), but it was regulative for the regenerate in certain concrete situations. It applies but to such; it was only laid on such. And even there in given circumstances. Its limitation is shown by the fact that Christ did not always follow it. He did not give to every asker. He would not answer every question; and the answers He gave were not always in love. There is nothing in it to regulate or explain Christ's treatment of the Pharisees, or His cleansing of the Temple, or His doom on Israel as a nation. As a matter of fact everybody makes his own selection from the Sermon. And it has no national reference at all. The precepts contained no guidance for nations. It was the Cross that dealt with the nation, taught nationality its place in the Kingdom of God, and consecrated judgment as a principle of national righteousness. The Sermon was less absolute than occasional. It did not legislate, and certainly did not in the air. It prescribed for special junctures, guiding the individual conduct of Christians in the face of religious persecution from the world; or it was for the guidance of the Church in certain of its internal affairs. But it has nothing to say on the relations of equal and self-governing nations where Christianity is formally acknowledged. It is not a sketch or manual of Christian ethic for all time and circumstance. It is more like the germinal *Bundesbuch* (Exod. xx. 22–xxiii. 33) of the New Testament; a small collection of case law, of precepts carrying in them great principles, and made for particular unrecorded junctures which were submitted to Christ within the individual or the Church life at an early stage; or they concerned the Christian's relation to a hostile pagan world, and not at all to the world of the Christian State more or less Christianised. It has a wealth of expansible meaning and duty in circumstances parallel to those present to Christ's mind, such as the religious persecution of an ideal Christian community. For instance, we have the precept 'Resist not evil.' Often the individual has shown how powerful non-retaliation is. But it is a wild leap from that to the 'martyr-State'—clearing much more than a thousand years in one day. Shall we interpret Christ's own Cross by that doctrine, and rob it of its active and positive effect, its national and universal range, by treating it as the supreme case of passive resistance? That is a fallacy which is destroying the Christianity of many at this moment, by reducing the Cross from a world-conquest to a soul's resigned martyrdom, and assigning a moral, and even a saving, value to sacrifice and death *per se*. But neither pain, nor death, nor sacrifice has saving value *per se*, but only according to its object. Christ did not atone by submitting to death, but by submission to death as God's judgment on sin; and He conquered death not by being put to death but by dying, and dying in deliberate obedience to a requirement in God. He laid down a life which could never have been taken from Him otherwise. His death was moral victory on a national, cosmic, eternal scale. The Cross has its value in its activity not its passivity to God's will, and in its activity in a national situation (as King of the Jews) on a world scale (as Son of Man) for righteousness unto blood (as Son of God). There are serious moral consequences, of a kind too quietist for the Kingdom of God, when we view the work of Christ on His Cross simply as an overpowering display of God's love to souls, and not also, and chiefly, as the confession and effectuation of God's righteousness in the same Act for a world. The present moral confusion of the pacifists is the *débâcle* of a view of the Cross which is more sympathetic than moral, and more devout than holy.[1] The Cross was meant to do much more than impress us, more even than to reconcile us. Its final bearing was its bearing on God, to whom it was chiefly offered. The Reconciliation rests on a moral Atonement set forth in blood, something that met a requirement of God whose holy urgency was greater even than the need of man. The Cross, by a holy war, sought first the righteousness of God, and only then and thereby, the wellbeing of man. The great public thing it did for man was to do justice to God's holiness in a nation's crisis, and, in the act, to destroy the evil power. Such is the love that melts us and fuses us in a Church. So the Cross-made Christian has not simply to consider his brother, but first his God. Our relation to the God of the universal and holy Cross is the foundation of all morality. There, in the practical faith of that Cross and the saving judgment in it, there, and in no preceptual conduct, lies the moral nerve of Christianity, and its creative ethic for the New Humanity. Death, viewed from the Cross, is not resigned suffering, and not impressive suffering.

[1] It is odd that some of the most 'tender' exponents of a sentimental religion are among the most belligerent critics of the pacifists they have been making for many years.

Christ did not die just to show how god-like a meek death could be made, nor even to show with the last emphasis how loving God is; but to hallow the Holy Name, to secure the real and universal righteousness, to destroy the work of the prince of this world, to judge him to death, and to set up the Kingdom of God on earth.

Everywhere the effect of death is an expression and an agent of God's righteousness reacting against sin; and in Christ's death it reacts to sin's destruction. By God's ordinance the wages of sin is death, or the horror of it. But death in itself could no more destroy the sin it dogged than suffering could. And in Christ we rise to a higher moral plane, and death acquires a new and nobler power. In His Cross we have a second reaction. We have there God's reaction upon death itself as the reaction on sin. If we should personify, Death itself, as an upstart servant and Jack-in-office, is slain, and its function is re-born. 'And death once dead there's no more dying then.' This was the war in heaven brought down to earth—not the abolition of death but its transcendence. And we also must react to death in this way if we die with Christ. We must take the nemesis and the terror out of it, and exploit it for God's glory. We must not cosset life, court immunity, or live for exemption. We are to react, at due call, and at the cost of life if need be, against unrighteousness, especially in its public and demonic forms. We are to do so by no mere passive resistance but actively, even if this course involve death or pain to ourselves or others. We are to destroy the aggressive works of the devil, even in blood. Did the crucified Christ make no war on Israel? Had He nothing to do with its national doom? If we are in Christ we are upon occasion to resist public evil, world-evil, inhuman evil, spiritual wickedness in high places, to the death whether of ourselves or of others. Christ, who was no martyr, made many. He cost them ease and life. He caused them suffering and death. So to resist evil, and destroy the work of the prince of the age, is to partake in Christ's intercession; which is not mere petition, but the energy of a soul poured out still in real action for the Kingdom of God among men and affairs.

That indicates the way in which the Cross is the fount and norm of Christian ethic, especially on its public scale. It must be so as the source of the *Holy* Spirit, searching to moral depths, filling a universal Church to be something else than a world-wide sect, and renewing all things that are done. It must be so as the source of the new birth and the new life on a universal and corporate scale—if that life is the moral life, the regenerate conscience, life not nursed in a retreat but spent in affairs, the new life of a world-righteousness in the Kingdom, the life that was born in a national crisis. To treat the Cross as only priestly, and for single souls, is to lose power out of it. To regard it as but a means of escape is to reduce it at last to the means of my escape only. It was priestly, but it was still more kingly, and therefore social and justiciary. He did not become a King by dying. He died as King—He said He did—taking order for the Kingdom and its righteousness in the world. That He sought first, for it involved all else—the New Humanity, the new heaven and earth. The treatment of Christ as priest suffered long from neglect of Christ as saint; and now Christ as saint becomes ineffectual, for lack of His due recognition as King, and His concern with history, with men in nations and realms. His death and resurrection, as the source of the new life, is the source of the universal ethic. It was the royal Act of world-righteousness in a national crisis, overcoming by warring unto blood. The moral nature of the source prescribes that of the course. The true destiny and ethic of history lies folded in the Cross, and in the regeneration there by and for holiness, by and for love's universal and absolute righteousness at any cost. It came not in a new commandment but in a new life—in a new *life*, a new power, quality, and principle, a holy energy of divine, historic, cosmic range, and not merely a new manner of life. The regeneration must be taken more seriously, searchingly, and radically than that, else let us get out of the way for the baptismal regenerationists, who are thorough enough on their wrong line. It must of course be taken more seriously than the rationalistic moralists do when they treat it as mere amendment. But it must also be taken with more moral seriousness than the sacramentarians do, who treat the new life as an influx rather than a birth, as a subconscious infusion into our nature rather than a radical change in the consents of our will and conscience. It is no mere subsidy, stimulant, restorative, or fresh impulse. It is a gift of life; yet of more than a mere spiritual vitality. The gift has a nature, and a nature which (being holy) is above all things moral and creative for the soul, and works mightily for righteousness in the moral relations and groupings of mankind. It was not a mere tonic. It was not merely a fresh draught of *élan*. It was nothing simply inbreathed to repair a flagging vitality, or act as an antiseptic to original sin. It was more revolutionary than that. It was a new moral birth. Only that, being moral, it was not unconscious as our natural birth is. At least it was not subconscious in the sense of being subliminal, but in the sense that the Act which saved the soul, being an Act of a compass which saved the whole world, was, in its moral range, beyond the grasp of the soul it saved. But for that soul it was newness of life from moral death. It was rescue from the death, the impotence, of sin. It was therefore moral re-creation by the Holy. It was effect given in the soul, by a creative revolution, for the moral ubiquity of the Holy, and His Self-establishment everywhere. It was the appropriation of His world-salvation. It came about not by a new wave of the old creation, but by a new Act of creation on a higher plane, by creation re-created, by a creation in its nature ethical, spiritually ethical, because holy. It was the source and principle, therefore, of the new life of the conscience and heart; it was not but a fresh charge of the old power to set us running again, and make the old car do its best with the old roads. And the second creation was at least as wide as the first. It was an act of fresh righteousness for the world, a quite new departure in that way, a creative thing with more love in it than led to the first creation, but righteous above all (Romans i. 17). And it settled the fate of the world in the historic crisis and doom of a nation.

Its moral products are in its own kind. *Vultus index animi.* They are holy love's native acts of world-righteousness. The new soul shall live and act on a world principle. Live and act on a principle good for all men who are in your case. The principle of the Cross for ethic is, therefore, something more than the primacy of individual love; it is the primacy and the final dominion of love as public righteousness in a Kingdom of God, even unto blood; it is the public and universal action of love; it has love's liberating action on the world's history through regenerate souls as a first charge on it. And still farther, it is something effected, and secured by central moral conquest once for all, and not merely so declared. The Cross was not there to show love in the sky over all, but to establish it for good in righteousness amid history. It is inadequate to say 'we must live out Christ's principle of forgiveness.' That way lies so much of our liberal futility. The principle of Christ's forgiveness was the principle of a gracious God's righteousness asserted for a world lost and secured as a divine Kingdom won. It can be lived out only by securing practically that type of righteousness in human affairs from the soul's centre outwards. Christ's first charge was not simply to forgive, to be a living channel of forgiveness, but to do practical justice and honour to the holiness of the Grace that forgave, and that even He did not procure. It was to give eternal life in righteousness. It was not to forgive without more ado, nor to produce a forgiving spirit, but to justify men, and to do so by a self-justification of the holy God. It was to forgive, moreover, by a national way that secured by active judgment, even through agony and blood, the great righteousness of the world and of Eternity. It was to effect the forgiveness of the Holy in a saving judgment that still acts as the deepest power hidden in God's detailed method with concrete history and its peoples. The Cross was a world event. It carries national effects, glories, and dooms. It is not a matter of private piety alone but also of public judgment. The consideration of the good, godly, and gentle spirits in Israel did not arrest Christ in the doom He knew He brought on the whole State. He did inflict A.D. 70. The prediction of a mere prophet became in Christ's mouth infliction from a Judge and King. It was not a view but a sentence when He spoke of the destruction of Jerusalem. He went to war with Israel by Cæsar, His satrap and servant. And if Christ judge the world, man, as he is in Christ, may and must do so in the hand of God. He is the commissary of the judgment of Christ, even when he deserves it not, nor even knows it.

The Cross is the source and norm of Christian ethic, public and private, in these respects among others :—

1. It was the destruction of egoism; and it was so in a national conflict. It broke, not nationality, but national egoism, which is idolatry. And it remains the grand power of the moral world for that purpose, whether in a national form or not.

2. It founded the final and universal principle

of the New Humanity on love's righteousness—and especially on the new righteousness of faith in Grace. It founded the great principle in which religion and ethic finally meet—justification by faith. What holiness is to love in heaven that righteousness is to love on earth. And the relation is less an analogy than a continuity.

3. It was and is the supreme revelation of the Holy, i.e. of the moral Absolute, as *the* active and decisive power in history. It was the source of the Holy Spirit, which at once goes to the soul's moral depths, and at the same time makes the social wealth of the universal Church among the peoples.

4. It contained the moral principle, therefore, of Judgment, and was indeed its effectuation on the whole scale of God and man. It was, in the deepest sense of the words, the last judgment. The wickedness of all the world was so judged on Christ that it is judged by Christ. It was so judged by His bearing of it that He mastered it, wielded it, and became by His Cross the Judge of all the earth, and the living Providence of the action of the final judgment in the nations. Such judgment is the grand moral principle of history—not in a negative way as retributory, but positively (and Scripturally) as the establishment of the righteousness of God's Kingdom, as the principle of the new creation.

These four heads make the substance of what I proceed to say, even if I do not follow their formal division. *And the heart of the whole matter is twofold—first, that the ethic of nationality is given by the Kingdom of God; and, second, that the Kingdom of God was set up in the Cross of Christ.*

Let us keep constantly in view the fact that Christ's 'finished work' was victory in a real moral conflict within His universal personality. If its nature was theological its manner was psychological. It ran through a dramatic history in His experience. It had what is called a moral pragmatism, a motivation more or less traceable in His holy consciousness. His soul had a history, and it also intended a historic Kingdom. It was, moreover, a history not only in contact with the history of His nation, nor only concentric with it, but identical with it. He was the soul of Israel's history, the 'truth' of it. The work of Jesus is the breath of prophecy. Israel came to itself in Him. His Cross acted deep below the nation's conscious centre, at its real core and true self. The proximate form in which He defeated the world and its egoism was national. And it was royal. He felt and said He was the true Israel. For Him Israel had been called into being, led, disciplined, and endowed. He was the King of the Jews. Egoism on His own part was lost in royalty —as it is in the One God, whose moral majesty it is to glorify His own name. He was really the Son of God that Israel had been poetically called. He not only saw, but He was, the Soul of Israel's divine history, all overlaid and falsified though it had come to be by the traditions of the fathers. These had come totally to misread the revelation that made the nation's vocation in the world, which it had changed from grace to force, and from witness to empire. Christ was not in His career working off a theological programme. That would have turned His life from real drama to histrionics. The drama in it was the drama of a nation, of history, the drama of humanity—of the last reality. It was all a real and moral conflict within His universal personality; and the form of it was prescribed by a national issue of righteousness. The whole deadly difference between Him and the Pharisees turned on their different interpretation of public righteousness. And the collision condensed, like our present war, a whole world issue for the New Humanity, and a striving unto blood. We may here think of His own blood which the nation shed as its end began, or their blood which His providential judgment shed, when the end came in the dreadful fall of Jerusalem.

His suffering, for instance, was very real. It was not æsthetic. He did not sit in ideal light and only feel the darkness of others. He did not use His immortality in such a way as made death to Him but a tunnel and not an abyss. He did not use His position as God's Son for privilege or immunity. He was not lifted by it to a bliss that left no room for pain. His suffering, sympathetic as it was, was not sympathetic only. He did not feel just what a kind heart would feel, only on an imaginative scale. He felt as only the Holy One could feel human evil. He felt sin as God felt it; and that was more than any fellowship of human pain. He never lost His sensibility for the moral situation—nay, for His own central place in it. So far from being always storm-free within, He was at last the storm centre, as He poured out His Soul unto a death which was God's curse upon sin. He saw and felt His death as the last judgment of His God, which He least of all could evade. He met it, but it was in no frame of mere courage, and certainly not as a superior person smiling down grief to a parterre of admirers. He met it with a fear and an agony which He conquered only by prayer, and in God's sight only, not man's.

Yet He suffered also as a citizen-Saviour, as an Israelite indeed, and the legatee of a unique historic past. In Him transpired the real tragedy of Israel's national soul. His agony was not superhistoric only. He was not rapt in another world.

It is said that Hegel, coming out of his house in Leipzig one day during the siege, was surprised to find the French in the streets. He had forgotten the investment of the place. No such unworldly reverie was an opiate to the Christ of the Passion. It may be true that His warfare was not with flesh and blood; that He was engaged in a mysterious battle in the Unseen; that He was at grips with Satan; that He was deep in the realisation of all the weight of the world's sin, and in the sense of God's wrath on it. But let us not in that conviction lose sight also of the historic realism of the situation, nor of His own sense of that. (Our religious individualism has beclouded all this to us, and made the very discussion of such things unintelligible.) There was enough in His personal experience to move Him to His depths, enough in the apparent collapse of His vocation as it seemed cut across by His death. The sense of the historic situation never left Him—the sense that He was putting His nation to the touch to win or lose all, and dooming in His death the race His whole effort had gone to love and save. Israel would not be severed from the Pharisees who had prussianised its religion. These were its gods. He was losing all the hopes to which He had given His life; and He envisaged all the doom He was bringing upon His people. He was its greatest and most fatal Lover. And how He loved them! 'Father, forgive them. They know not what they do.' That was not for the ignorant executioners, but for the murderers, for Israel. Yet the prayer, even His prayer, was not granted. He must go to war and judgment on this people, and He must entail, not to say inflict, its defeat and ruin in blood. His life was a process of disillusioned love, whose reality He came to find but in service, suffering, and death, and not in the enjoyment of success. But He did find reality and life there. The love of the Father whose will it was did not fail Him. If His Father forsook Him His groan never challenged the righteousness in it. Hence, though He could be bitter, He was never embittered, and never desperate. He was a patriot, but the patriot of Israel's true mission against Israel's egoism and empire. It was God's Kingdom against world empire. He not only saw His people making the greatest mistake a nation could commit, but He was the occasion of it. He, their Saviour, was the stumbling-stone on which they broke. He was forcing the issue in which a people that was religious or nothing was sealing its doom by mistaking its God, and misreading that revelation of Him whose custody gave the nation its only right to be. It was, for the then Church, the same fatal blunder which, at a later date, made inevitable the Reformation and all its train; the like blunder by which the Church, become incurably canonical, seized on the wrong element in its Bible, and chose the ritual and sacramental factor in the New Testament instead of the prophetic and evangelical. It had become priestly at the cost of its apostolicity. Christ's whole charge against the Pharisees was that they had done the same with their Bible as God's Word. A veil was on Moses' face that the more people might look, and the most miss the glory. Observance had engrossed their obedience and stupefied their soul. Rabbinism had quenched insight, as philology might literature, or as a clericalism kills apostolic succession. That was why they could not recognise or own Him when He came as the real burthen of prophecy. He came as the soul of a live national righteousness which they had reduced to rabbinism. He was the true Gospel of a catholic book which they had turned to a mere propaganda. So when He was not meaningless to them He was exasperating. His Gospel for a world made a crisis for His people. He had to press that crisis to the far end. And in doing so he had to take a step which involved the giving up, not of 'life's minor hopes or desires which mean so much to those without vocation,' but what had seemed His national vocation till now. He had to see His great Messianic æon sink in blood, and feel it all to be the result of His prophetic action to His people. He could not till the last moment settle to the certainty that the intelligible way of the Messianic King was fruitless, and that the unintelligible doom of the Cross was God's will and way for Him—though living or dying He was His Father's. The Cross presented itself as it had often loomed on Him—as the end and ruin of Messiah's work, or at least of its first gracious form—the preaching of God's Sovereignty of Grace and Fatherhood. But now for Israel Grace, perverted into force, turned to judgment. His passion to preach repentance to His nation was now cut across by a certainty of judgment on it which left no place for repentance, but only tragedy and ruin. The conviction had long been growing in Him, it now came to a sure head. He never doubted indeed that God would prevail. But He had to realise that God's last gift to Him was the failure of all on which He had spent His life in the hope of saving at least the better Israel from its hard taskmasters. The hope was vain. The people had been taught too long and too skilfully, and had been debased too much. They had chosen their masters and lost their soul. The Cross confessed the national failure of the most royal prophetism, of all Christ's work in that vein. For Israel was impenitent. It was rusted into its bonds. It was hardened beyond the possibility of salvation. There remained but its collapse. And He must not evade the Cross, which began in His blood the end which was completed in theirs. He must not stand aside from this judgment, let it go past Him, do nothing, seek retreat, and leave God to work a miracle if He would avert bloodshed and ruin. That were tempting God and deserting Him. He inflicted on Israel His death and all that that entailed. He did the one imperative thing. He so went to judgment as to become their judgment, and He left the historic result to God. His blood was on them and their children. And in all this Israel stood to His mind for the race.

The New Israel was the New Humanity—not denationalised, but with its nations bright in their setting in the family of peoples and the Kingdom of God.

It cannot be right to ignore as we do the fact that Christ's work of Reconciliation was conducted by a sharp unsparing polemic, a national polemic, the greatest polemic the world has ever seen—the war of the Kingdom of God against its nation chosen and fallen. The Cross, when taken profoundly enough, supplies the lack which has been charged against Christianity of having no public ethic. It is the source of national morals as well as private—the Sermon is not.

The action of a nation is not the mere parallel of the individual's on a larger scale, though it is the postulate of individual action and its medium. Therefore the source of social, and especially of State, morality is different in kind from that which might suffice for stray individuals. It is not precept. It is divine action, ending one age and creating a new. It is equally real with law, but ampler in its wealth and power. It comes from the heart of a great historic and divine event, from a national revelation, with a reference both individual and cosmic. It comes from the place of the Cross of Christ in Israel and its function there for the Kingdom of God. That Cross was the crisis of an ethical nation's doings, and the focus of that nation's doom. It has the secret in it of a nation's moral soul, and the principle of a nation's place in the Kingdom of God, i.e. of a nation's ethic, and of the judgment in that ethic. Christ did indict a nation. He declared war on it (though not on its nationality) to His own death, and to His people's final doom in blood. He moved against a nation deeply religious, but whose religion had sunk to a fierce, proud, and pious patriotism, thirsting for the mastery of the world.[1] It had fallen into the hands of those who would sacrifice the whole people to that ambition. It had therefore become a non-moral religion, and thereby the enemy of the Kingdom of God. It was not the 'immorality' in the sinners of Israel that Christ encountered, despaired of, and judged to death and blood. It was the immorality of respectable, cultured, and religious Israel. It was a Pharisaism which had captured the Bible and the people, and so misread its own charter and mission as to substitute national dominion for holy grace, and therefore for ethic, in public affairs. Israel had become the vassal of Pharisaism, with a military hero, Messiah, and Superman, and an iron law laid on humanity and freedom. Such righteousness Christ called sin, and such good evil. The system was radically, mortally, wrong for Him. Pharisaism had many virtues and much culture as these things go. It was able, thorough, accurate, even punctilious, and devoted to a national ideal. But it had no insight nor faith, and therefore it was rotten. Its burthen was the culture of its *Thorah*—of life systematised and policed. The nation that fell to that system, that religious prussianism I have called it, was judged in Christ's blood upon it and its children. It was doomed to perish at the hands

[1] May I refer to my article in the *Contemporary Review*, June 1916, on the 'Conversion of the Good'?

of a more efficient form of that imperialism whose cult had blinded its eyes to Himself. Christ declared war on theocratic Israel, not on Rome—as we do on Christian Germany and not on pagan Japan. The worst antagonism may be where there is most in common. God quenched for ever His own Israel. Judgment begins at the house of God—to the scandal of those charitables who deplore warfare more than wickedness.

Christ found Israel more antichrist than Rome. Yet He did not raise and lead an army against Israel. That is not God's way. He sets evil against evil, dividing Satan's house against himself, making the war of man to praise Him. He found the instrument of His judgment to His hand in Rome. Rome was His sword and scourge, as Assyria had been. The Roman Empire, unsaintly as it was, was the agent of God's providence for purposes both of law and arms, of peace and war, of blessing and judgment. It was both His staff and rod. He certainly used that Jewish war for His righteousness, setting evil against evil. It was His holy judgment on Israel's moral crime. It was part of His providential ethic. And it was none the less so that it was worked out by a moral necessity, that the same demented moral temper which slew Christ made its desperate and infatuate throw against Rome. From His Cross He ruled that war in His saving providence for history. It was the Cross that doomed Israel. At any rate Christ did not shirk the full moral issue, nor did He draw back because it involved the personally guiltless in desolation and blood for righteousness' sake. He did not cease to beard the rulers of His people's darkness, nor hold His hand because the Pharisees were truly religious, godlier than Cæsar, and had more in common with Himself. It is not always with those with whom we have most in common that we most agree; they may hold the truth in unrighteousness. Christ's holy love did not evade a crisis charged with misery and death to the innocent and the unborn. It would be more true to say He forced it. For all His love of His people He did not retire from strife with the kind of religion that had captured them. He did not spare them because some among them represented the best and most earnest religion of the time. This must be remembered when we are told of the deep religion in Germany. It is religion pious, but de-ethicised below even its own deep knowledge. It is religion content with Prussia and Belgium. It is religion whose Church has never raised a voice against the national massacre of innocents, though it has in it some of the most valuable authorities on Christian ethic of an academic kind. It is religion that gave all its children a holiday for the 'Lusitania.'

Christ did not go out of public action because of the good men whom He was involving in Israel's doom; nor did He retreat from His aggressive treatment of His rebels and slayers, and betake Himself to a long life of prayer, and to the quiet influencing of groups who might leaven the future. He did not take the pietist line, forswear national action, and leave God to work a miracle to save His Kingdom. It is not so hard to exchange the moral for the miraculous. It relieves us of the coward's dread—responsibility. Many will endure martyrdom for an opinion for one who will take responsibility in a great venture. He carried to the bitter end His war with an Israel whose egoism, for all its virtues, served Satan more than God. He became the national doom who had been the nation's victim. And He did so in view of all it meant for national misery. His work was not to avert judgment—He even took it on Himself, He let it fall on Him. Nor was His object to refuse to act as the instrument of judgment in God's hand. For it was His agony to know that the Cross He freely went to was to be His nation's curse. But His purpose was to convert judgment both in the endurance and in the exercise of it, to turn a nation's doom to a world's boon. Judgment falling on goodness like His, on such love of man, on such obedience, such passion for righteousness, and such practical confession of God's holiness, became redemptive. And such Redemption, as it is our chief gift, becomes our chief responsibility and therefore our chief judgment. He converted condemnation to salvation, and made judgment the agent of love and its atonement; which is a far greater moral achievement than to go round it, take the gentle way, and win the winsome fame. (It is high time to moderate our application of dainty terms like winsome to the crushed sin-bearer, the Judge of all the earth, and the antagonist of the prince of the world. Even in His Resurrection glory He is something else than winsome.) But in the Act He became our Judge. This stone, if we do not fix it on our chief corner, falls upon us, and breaks us to powder. God Himself uses force at last from the very Cross, and gives it its moral place within a Christian ethic whose source is there. The love that lifts life, that sweetens, fortifies, and hallows it, is also a consuming fire.

We may pause here to notice again that facile view of salvation which, by abolishing judgment and eliminating atonement, reduces the freeness of redeeming grace to a revealed amnesty or suffusion of love which simply deifies paternal affection. This, the favourite theology of the public has done for half a century. This creed is now working out its ethical consequences in a decay of moral virility, or of moral realism on an imaginative scale. It might, to the passing glance of a mere reader, seem a piece of extravagance to connect the Atonement with a national ethic or with public affairs at all. But it is really their disconnection that has been the bane of religion for public effect. It is a real Atonement that really ethicises Christianity. This is a point which it is impossible to elaborate here. But it may seem less absurd if, being prepared to admit that the starting-point of all theology is the holiness of God, we notice that that places an absolute and mystic ethic in command of all things. The Atonement was the founding of God's Kingdom among the nations in the practical meeting by a historic Christ of the requirement of that sublimated righteousness which we call the holiness of God in His kingdom. To holiness the idea of judgment is even more essential than that of sacrifice, which is associated rather with love. So that if God is holy love the Cross is a judgment sacrifice. And if we are fellow-workers with God we must not shrink from executing judgment any more than from making sacrifice. We must make sacrifices to execute God's judgment, even if we feel no more worthy than was Cyrus His servant. The elimination of this central and public conscience in Christianity takes shape in the conventual pacifism of devout groups, whose idealist faith has parted with the tonic of judgment, and whose ethic has another centre and a poorer quality than the world-righteousness of the Holy One's Cross. Theological error about the core or source of an ethical religion always works out in time into moral failure at a crisis correspondingly great. And this present crisis is one where nothing less than the principle of a holy and righteous Redemption of a world in the blood of Christ will serve as moral guide.

I heard a remarkable phrase lately, used to reprove those who thought that the whole Christian issue for history was involved in the war, and that because of it the Kingdom of God was struck in the face. 'As if because of the war God's Kingdom had ceased to go on.' Certainly God will see that His Kingdom does go on. But that great faith was not what underlay the phrase. What did underlie it was a greater interest in the evangelisms, reforms, and benevolences of the societies and committees than in the moral issue of nations at the core of the long tragedy of history. It was the spirit of historic detachment which keeps a sect a sect. It was a greater concern for the benevolent business of the Church than in the imperial business of the Kingdom of God. It betrayed a frame of mind which has much, if not everything, to do with the present ineffectual state of religion. Is the Kingdom of God concrete with history and public affairs in such a way that if things went wrong at a world juncture and a moral issue like the present it would receive one of the greatest blows in Time, from which no benevolence could recover us? Or is that Kingdom of such a nature that its subjects and its efforts might go on at religious business as usual, with a minor concern about the war, its moral inwardness, and its practical issue for the whole world? Would it be but partially and indirectly, but not substantially, affected by our defeat, so long as the atmosphere and work of, for instance, American Christianity, or the Keswick Convention, or the Swanwick Conferences, or the May Meetings went on? Luther taught us to carry religion into our life's vocation, and said that business was no less sacred in its nature than monkery, and lent itself no less to the Kingdom of God. But there is a kind of protestant monkery, cultivating a religion of coteries, the ideas of a cave, with benevolence of a merely individual kind, and moving in a bustle of organisations which are apt to be but littleness writ large. Truly it is a blessed work; but it can be a blinding unless it is carried on a creed as large as its desire. These cloistered circles tend to become more or less indifferent to the great historic and national movements of the Spirit, or indeed to any public issues, unless these affect the obvious moralities of Villadom, or some religious programme more ambitious than catholic. Neither Luther nor his Church has carried his valuable principle into their own national life; which has accordingly been captured for a commercialism that despises the Church, but lusts to capture the world, a militarism that expressly flouts the Kingdom of God and the humanities of men, and a policy that renounces moral control at choice. But the more a nation escapes from mere force, and becomes a State with a system of law and right, the more does it acquire moral personality. Such a State corresponds in a nation to personality in the individual. And accordingly it has the vocation of all moral personality to serve God, and seek first the righteousness of His Kingdom in history. There are in the Cross of Christ ranges of righteousness for that Kingdom whose scope transcends the limits of the individual, but are in some parity with the compass of State action. A State may or may not establish a Church, but it is morally bound to establish the Kingdom of God in its conduct with other States, and to carry out that righteousness with other nations. In that service it is bound to serve God's historic principles and purposes, even to the point of acting as His agent of judgment at need. It may have to police on due occasion the peoples that abjure, in profession or conduct, His realm of righteousness and humanity, and that stand in the world for 'absolute war,' war, that is, with no consideration moral or human. This, however, is an aspect or function of the historic Cross which has been neglected by a domestic evangelicalism, a too homely ethic, a too personal pietism, or a sentimental liberalism of mere fraternity—to the cost of the public influence of the whole of those types of religion. In the pacifist movements we have this monkery, this non-nationalist religion, going on to a religion anti-nationalist, rather than supernationalist. We have amateur ethic, and a religion disinherited of the long history of its public either in Church or State. We have a conventicle Christianity without weight with the public because without moral nerve or insight on a world scale, a theological scale. We have, emerging into sight and effect, the difference between a Church Christianity and a group Christianity, between a Christianity founded on the evangelical ethic of a new creation of the historic conscience in the holy Cross and a Christianity founded on a natural ethic of atomic conduct re-published by Christ with a new impetus in His fine personality and precept. The whole group type has an anti-national tendency, from which the sects only escape when they grow, by the evangelical range of conscience, out of mere societies into true Churches. It lives in pools that the sea has left, in religious backwaters and unhistoric juntos. In a book I published in 1912 entitled 'Faith, Freedom, and the Future,' I tried to call attention to what seemed to me the neglected fact that Independency was the product of two factors—the intimate, energetic, but scrupulous Anabaptism of Germany, driven through Holland to England, and the controlling Calvinism of the stately Puritans. It was the stiffening of Calvinism that saved the sectary element from sinking into the sand as it did elsewhere, and made the Free Churches. But the theological element has gone for the hour, with its binding, steadying, and majestic ethical strength, and with it has gone our rule by the evangelical principle. The spiritualistic element is left to its head in certain idealists, and it takes its conventiclist effect against the idea and ethic which make and mark a Church, whether that effect take the shape of neologism at one time or of pacifism at another. The public reaction from the pacifism of groups (whether ethical, pious, or rationalist) will, at a later point, be a great asset for the national Church. The Free Churches will, however unreasonably, be stamped with the group stigma, owing to the scope they give for honeycombs of devout fellowship, too cellular and too sweet. I say such a stigma would be unreasonable because such groups are but sporadic in the general tone. They are not without much value for religious elevation, but in ethic they do less to brace and guide.

If it be asked whether the line of discussion is not wandering somewhat afield from the matter of Christian ethic I may repeat myself to the inquirer thus. What holiness is to love in heaven that righteousness is to love on earth. And the connection is much more than an analogy; it is really a continuity—holiness continuing in heavenly conditions the righteousness in earthly affairs, and the same love being the bond of heaven as is the bond of heaven and earth. Therefore we do not ramble when we speak of the great Atonement by holiness to the holiness of God as being the foundation of all the ethic of righteousness on earth, and the principle of all judgment on men and all justification of man before God.

CHAPTER X

JUSTIFICATION AND JUDGMENT

How is ethic, and especially national ethic, connected with a piece of religion so theological as Justification by Faith? The answer to that question is not simple but it would take this line. The doctrine represents the moral feature which lifts the Christian Reconciliation above the level of a mere composition with the divine Creditor. The moral quality of Christ's supreme work is shown by the fact that the same Act which reconciles us is also our justification; and it is farther shown by our justification having moral goodness not as its mere sequel, but as its object. As Wernle says: it is in the doctrine of justification that Christian theology and Christian ethic meet. Our faith is neither an assent nor a sensibility; it is our life answer in kind to an Act which made us really righteous, and not but piously —righteous in a quite new and living way, attuned to God's higher will. We are placed by that Act (if we will) in a new order of righteousness called the Kingdom of God, which is really the Sovereignty of God, and means a vital relation to Him and His holiness more than a compliance or an organisation. It is quite other than legal or preceptual, being a matter of life, and of ever deeper life, in a personal relation with the Holy and His love. Our small and turbid streams, full of such sound and fury, are received into a world-righteousness of love and life eternal, whose moving waters flow in pure ablution round earth's human shores, and which salves and completes the partial justice or goodness of earth. We are caught up with all our loose ends, and woven into the goodness not of a decalogue but of a Christ. We are ingrafted into a holy, and only therefore changeless, love, whose first concern is cosmic and eternal righteousness, and which chastises without ceasing to love; for our Lover is our Holy One, Who for His holiness spared not even His Son.

The tissue of history has two sides, an upper and an under. On the upper side the pattern is clear and complete, on the under it is ragged and dim. On the upper side the eye of God alone rests Who sits at the loom of Time, on the under side our gaze is turned. We therefore decipher the design with difficulty, and, where the pattern is fine, not at all. But it is given to us, looking up beyond the edge of this canopy, to see in a glass what the Weaver sees always. We see condensed and reflected, as in a concave mirror in the heavens, the large lines of the scheme and even the denouement. We see there, in a small but finished form, the purpose which on the seamy side of the fabric is but in blurred and uncouth shape. We see not yet all things working out the Kingdom, but we see Jesus. But it is the same righteousness, His righteousness, on both sides of the historic web. Perfect heavenward in Christ, it is but striving to be articulate on its earthly side, through the confusion of the history we see. It is struggling to the Kingdom of God. The upper side is the righteousness of the Kingdom come and sure, the under is that of the Kingdom coming, the realm of historic judgment and justice. The former is the region of faith, the latter of sight. We are in the former by our personal faith, in the latter by our public works. The one is the realm and range of the eternal fulness, the other the realm of the same spirit, but humiliated to man and his procession of strife. The one is the land of love in possession, the other of love in its agony. But it is the same love, holy and irresistible. The righteousness that reigns with Christ in heaven is the same righteousness that wrestles in historic affairs for judgment and mercy, sweating great drops of blood. The conflict of the nations, within or without, is the action and ferment of the Kingdom of God, whose new wine bursts the old bottles. But by faith we open and drink in that Kingdom.

Therefore to men of faith (and not of sentiment or æsthetic) this world-righteousness must be, in public matters, the first charge on their love; which love aims, accordingly, at placing all men in that final good, whether nationally by just liberty, or personally by holy faith. For a Christian nation, like a Christian soul, owes its last right to be to its place and function in the Kingdom of God. Love, when we pass beyond instinctive or domestic limits, and when we enter its historic Christian principle, is the desire to see our neighbours in the possession of their best right, dignity, and liberty, which is a common life in the loving and saving righteousness of God. The more wide and public its range, the more it becomes the righteousness of the Kingdom. We are saved, whether as souls or nations, in a Church and Kingdom where the mighty matter is love—but love in the form of a real world-righteousness and a passion to set all men and peoples there, in heart, conscience, and condition, to the glory of God the Father. It may or may not take the form of individual affection. And it does not ignore the wrath, the judgment, of God.

We are justified moreover by faith in this cosmic righteousness not as a mere ideal (with its impatience) but as a foregone achievement of God in spiritual places, on which we rest and in patience win our soul. It is the loss of this moral and final idea of justification, the replacement of its faith either by an unhistoric mysticism or by a mere idealism, dropping to religious naturalism—it is this that is the cause of the worst weakness and the most placid demoralisation in recent and popular versions of Christianity. In such a way that love, stripped of its moral element of intrinsic and inalienable holiness, subsides into sympathy alone, and ends in sentiment and a sentimental virility. The Cross of Christ, ceasing to be related to the holiness of God by any Atonement, ceases to be moral at the core. It ceases to be the ground of our justification, i.e., the source of our new morality, which we think to find in a mere and simple fatherhood of pity and benediction, without judgment unto victory. The Cross becomes but the exhibition of fatherhood at a particular call on it instead of a constituent element in it;

it becomes an impressionist device instead of an act of real judgment. Or it is viewed as the great outcrop of the sacrificial and redemptive principle in the first creation, instead of a constant element in the holy fatherhood of the second, and due to the Father's holiness even more than to the children's need. Thus, by the loss from our Christian faith of the religious experience and the moral theology of justification, we lose also the principle of Christian ethic as rooted in a holiness eternal and a judgment unto forgiveness. It becomes a sequel rather than the element of our salvation. And we become the victims of all kinds of susceptible sympathies, or of an idealist and ineffectual conscience which is more apt in asserting its own freedom than in divining the righteousness of God, and feeling His way in this jungle of a world with the woodcraft of the Spirit. Christian ethic is a theological ethic. There is but one ethic, which is the Christian; and it has but one source—the Cross of the Holy Love. And the doctrine of justification by faith carries within it the moral principle and spiritual badge of this supremely ethical religion for man as he actually and morally is—man in families and nations within a Kingdom of God.

The ethic of Christian faith, therefore, has a first regard to the eternal righteousness of God's historic Kingdom for the New Humanity, built on the foundations of the historic and atoning Cross. The first interest met by God's love is righteousness—if the Cross reveal that love as holy, if it is the atoning Cross of our Justification. Our new righteousness was in Christ's blood. The Atonement was the crisis of the 'war in heaven,' of God's moral warfare with man. Human righteousness came by that offering and joy given to God's righteousness, and prolonged in us by the indwelling action of the Holy Crucified and Risen. It was and is by the mortal obedience, surrender, and reparation of the Holy to the Holy. It was under the suffering conditions of a holy yet historic war. But always (I keep urging) the world-righteousness of the Holy One was first (Romans i. 17), at any cost of either suffering or death (2 Cor. v. 21). That requirement of God was the first thing in Christ's last thoughts, and took precedence of man's need. God Himself paid the price (the Father suffering, maybe, more than the Son), but paid it must be; judgment there must be, but a judgment where deaths teem with moral life. And there, in that divine and racial Act, lies the creative principle of Christian life and ethic—especially of its more public and historic forms. The larger our scale of action the more does love take this historic form of righteousness at any cost, and the Kingdom at any price. The Cross shows that the public form of love is righteousness—sympathetic righteousness, first with God, and then with man. It is for each soul a concrete, historic, actual, and social righteousness working out into the world, because the Cross was not shown in the air but inserted in the tissue of history, with the eloquence and action of affairs. It involved the Roman Empire, as was shown in due course when it took possession of it. The Cross was organic with human history, and

Christ with the New Man. Its ethic therefore is not trivial, ethereal, nor aloof, but concrete with affairs. As soon, for instance, as a war passes beyond the tussle of two peoples, as soon as it becomes a world-conflict not only by its area but by the moral quality of its issue for humanity, as soon as one side disowns all moral control and humane conduct at national choice, and thus makes its enemies the champions of conscience and humanity—then love, if it is divine, goes to a Cross, takes up the form and function of righteous judgment, and resists unto blood. It is not as if we had a realm of providence in the first creation with a realm alongside it of redemption in the second, and the inscrutable calamities in the one were just meant to cast us over the frontier into the other, there to shelter till the storm was overpast. That is a crude and maimed conception of the divine action, and lacks its unity of plan. But the first creation with its providential course was made for the second, and only comes home in it, though by the way of creation and not evolution, of redemption and not mere development. Conversely the second creation has all along been reacting on the first and moulding it. Nature, if not the mother, is the matrix of Grace. Salvation is the ground plan of creation, and the *primum mobile* of Nature itself. And it is from the second creation and its new birth that the last powers and initiations proceed which subdue the prepared ways of the first to its control, as the goal is rest after strife. The whole creation creaks and groans for the manifestation of the crucified Son of God, and the bringing forth of His judgment unto victory.

No one can dwell on the inwardness of these mighty matters without feeling the effect of a current which sets against him from the mentality of the present age. He is suspected, or charged, with getting so far away from what the modern mind deems reality that his whole line of thought is treated as lucubration. The whole *modus operandi* in a matter like justification is regarded as too abstract and too artificial, too forensic for simple religion or the plain conscience—though when a man needs justification most his religious condition is anything but simple, and his conscience anything but plain.

And one of the oldest and most obvious objections to the doctrine of justification is its moral unreality. If God (it is said) can count right a man who is wrong, and has not yet amended his life, that destroys our idea of God by its moral falsity. There is illusion somewhere, incompatible with moral clarity. And no doubt if justification is not fundamental it is fallacious.

The answer is that the objection treats God as an observer, a thinker, a critic, forming a certain estimate of us on a divine survey of our merits. But that is not the Christian relation between Him and us. For religion it is not a question how we think of God; and so it is not a question of how God thinks of us, how He reckons us up. Were it so, there could of course, with a perfectly holy God, be no such thing as justification. But it is not a question of His thought of us; it concerns His will toward us. It is a matter not of verdict but of treatment, not of a judgment He forms of us but of a judgment He exercises on us. The unreality comes from treating a personal relation as a mere case of connection, observation, and decision. If you treat your neighbour, who is a living will, merely as an object of inquiry and estimate, with mere logic and its conclusions, you are unnatural and unreal, morally unreal. You are not handling a moral reality in a moral attitude, with the moral method. And to transfer such an attitude to our God is to introduce moral unreality there. It is to demoralise religion. The justice of God is not justice of mind but of personality. It is not mere assessment of us, it is something more sympathetic, something creative. His judgment on man is creative judgment, the creative judgment of the Holy, saving and sanctifying judgment, judgment which always views its own sanctity as the destiny of all, and which makes the thing it misses in that direction. It is not a judgment merely critical. Its notice of what is wrong is but the condition and passion for setting it right. This is the nature of God's righteousness as given us in Christ, Who is the great moral reality of the world, and the moral principle deepest in its life and action. In this self-revelation of His moral holiness, God took the field as the forgiving and redeeming God; for holiness was there not simply displayed for adoration by those sensitive to it, but it was established in command of humanity in a Kingdom. And holiness cannot be established except by making men holy—which was done in Christ as the creative Surety of their future, and not merely its dawn or its prophet. We are His entail and not merely His sequel. That is His will, His supreme righteousness—a forgiveness which is also Eternal Life, and which overcomes and commands the concrete world. Our supreme righteousness is to meet this great deed and gift. That is faith. Faith is meeting God's holy forgiveness in kind. It is responding to His righteous mercy and its last judgment. When we live by that, we live by the supreme moral reality, we come to our moral selves. Redemption is the most royal thing we know in God; and man's royalty is his loyalty to it. It is more royal than conscience. The conscience really loyal meets that Grace with faith in it, with self-committal. There can be no unreality in trusting the saving righteousness of God, and there can be nothing immoral in answering this great Act of His holy love in kind. Our evangelical faith is doing supreme justice to a God Who, because holy, must establish holiness in command everywhere, Who, therefore, is supreme as Saviour, Who is just and the Justifier, Who judges iniquity out of being, Who is righteous even to the pitch of holiness in all the ways of His love, and to our redemption into it. Indeed it is the one means of putting right all that is wrong with us. The man of perfect faith in God's Grace is right with that supreme will of God. He is the man made for the divine image, made to reflect God, the man of the normal personality, the personality for which he was earmarked by a God holy enough in His judgment of us to redeem us into a holiness to which we had failed to grow. Faith is the divine destiny of free beings created for righteousness by holy love. We were born to be redeemed, and to believe in our redemption into this holy and active righteousness; which is not compliance with injunction but response to a person. Faith is not a second best; as if the absolute best would have been sinless obedience to instructions, correct attention to orders, or even full trust in a lovable person, who yet might not have power in His love to redeem. There are moral resources in God and His holiness which nothing but our sin and Redemption draw out. So far, *O felix culpa!* And these reserves are the deepest—the resources of Grace, of which He was well aware in Himself when He created man free to sin. Only the mighty to save could make us free to fall. To meet, and confess, and hallow in action that deepest thing in God is the greatest thing we can do as men. The greatest moral act of which man is capable in worshipping obedience to God's holy grace. That is our faith. That is what it does. The trust of Grace is greater than the obedience that never strayed from Love and knows no repentance. It is a greater God that redeems than just blesses; and to trust Him as Saviour is therefore the greatest work possible to the soul. The praise of men is greater than that of angels.

When we really close with the question, is there more moral unreality in Justification than in any contact of a holy God with guilty man? If we gauge it, that is a thing more startling than war. If we are ever to be in any right relation to God, it must now be amid our sin. We have behind us, the race has behind it, a mass of sinful acts or experiences which go to form the actual and concrete situation. Yet we meet with God's mercy and answer it. But if He thus come out to us and consent to touch us, if such as we have access to a holy person at all, if we ever worship Him, it is touching Him with our sinful personality. Is there not, on the critic's hypothesis, a moral unreality there—in any friendly contact of the Holy with the sinful? Could the Holy One simply forget His Holiness? It would be forgetting Himself. Could He forget our treatment of it? Can the past be undone and be as if it had never been? Impossible! Unreal! This is only mentioned here to show that the difficulty in Justification by faith is not a theological cobweb, but it is the question of all religion in proportion as it is seriously taken and morally. The mystery of Justification is the mystery of a holy God and the sinful soul altogether, when that mystery is thoroughly faced. And it is a mystery solved only by an atoning redemption and the new creation in it. Exactly how, how He can forgive fully and be absolutely holy, that is the mystery of Atonement. It was certainly not done in exchange for what Christ brought; for He came from Grace, He did not procure it. If the first creation is a mystery the second is a miracle. Religion has no existence except as the answer to Revelation; Christian religion is the answer to Revelation as Redemption and Regeneration. True and living religion is the answer to true and creative Revelation, a Revelation which makes us over again. But for Christianity Revelation is holy love at issue with sin. It is therefore holy Grace, when we come to the point with Christ and His Cross. Real religion, therefore (if the real is the moral), is the answer to such Grace. But the answer to Grace free and infinite is neither character nor conduct (which would still be achievement, and so would limit Grace) but it is faith in Grace absolute. It is a man meeting and trusting a gracious God for everything, for his very Atonement. It was to create such faith that God gave Himself in revelation, to make a new man, not to patch the old. It was not to enlarge the old goodness but to create a new type of goodness, and a higher—higher because the second creation reflects a deeper interior in God than the first did. If we come to our true selves as we rise to our destiny in creation it is by our response to this new creation. Behind and within the first creation there was always the second as a greater creation still, a greater thing in the way of creation than the first. It is the new creation in faith that gives us our truest selves, and makes us completely right with God's holiness, which was not revealed in the first creation at all. We are only really, finally, morally right only as God's Grace has its way with us, as the immoral thing, sin, is judged, doomed, and replaced by the moral thing, faith—faith moralised by its holy object. The deeper righteousness of God is revealed as we go on from faith to faith, from natural faith to supernatural and not simply as we rear by conduct and culture the moral personality. It might perhaps obviate some difficulties if we were more exact in our language, and spoke of Justification by Grace as regeneration, and Justification by faith as conversion.

God's judgment-Grace to sin is His supreme action as righteousness. He is never so true to His Holy Self and law as in that Atonement. It may indeed be for us the supreme problem. Like purging war we should never have expected it in His world. It is the matter and miracle of His revelation, the union in Grace of holy law and holy love, of holy God and evil man. The precise mode of adjustment, its ultimate moral inwardness, is something He has reserved in His own hands to a large extent. Yet so that He should be inquired of. It is of the Holy Spirit that we make our theories of Atonement. They are part of our worship of the Act and Fact. They are another phase of the theology of miracle. They are our efforts to penetrate the mystery on the note and the impulse He has given in His revelation of reconciliation. But at least we know that the deep divine relation to the world is one of moral crisis rather than evolution. And crisis is judgment. The crisis of the Cross is the moral centre and principle of the world, the Act that makes a new moral universe; and the response to it is our answer in kind to the last moral reality, which underlies all creation, all history, all the movements of men in nations, though they be as terrible as the national crucifying of the Son of God.

Faith is a life, and therefore a righteousness. It is not merely an experience, nor a single act, far less a forced act, but it is a life-act. That is, it is an act, before all else, of the will and conscience which make personality, with all the power and glory of Christian love latent in it, and only possible through it. It is a life in a direct union of trust (and not fusion) with God as the God of holy love. Truly the foundation of Christian ethic is love. But it is God's love, not man's—God's holy grace, not man's lovely romance. It is much more than human desire, or sympathy, or passion. It does not rest on man's love to man amiable or needy, and it is not ruled by it; but it rests on God's love to whatever He loves most. And what He loves most is not His prodigal, nor even His saint, but His Son. He loves most the perfect and perpetual reflection of His Holiness in His eternal and delightsome Son, in whom His satisfaction is eternal. 'Not for your sakes do I this but for my Holy Name, which ye have defiled.' God's love, as distinct from man's, is holy, and it has therefore a place and need for judgment as man's has not. To deify man's love gives one religion, to trust God's is another. And the latter is religion as revealed and as Christian. It founds on the self-revelation of the Holy Love acting and reacting amid sin. Its prime concern, as revealed in the holy Cross, is with blood-won righteousness in a world kingdom, a kingdom of souls, a historic kingdom, whose being is among the nations though its fulness is in heaven. Heaven is its continuation and completion, it is not its contrast. God's Kingdom is not of this world, but it is *for* it. And God's love is His love to man, but to *sinful* man. It acts to evil man in the only way in which the Holy could love him, in the way of redeeming the race, through its history, for that holiness, and by the way of that righteousness. It is in that righteousness, historic and racial, that every soul is saved. It is in the action of that moral love in its blood. But if man is redeemed in that love, by and for that historic righteousness, the historic form of his Christian ethic corresponds to its fount. It is prescribed by the form taken by that holy love in the historic redemption of the world. And that form, while it is truly sacrifice, is not sacrifice only (which may or may not be good) but also blessed judgment—an offering and a sacrifice not alone for man but also to righteousness, to glorify not man but God's holy name in its severe and saving reaction on human sin. Moreover, it took effect in a national crime, the shirking of God's national call; its action therefore cannot be irrelevant to national conduct and destiny. It is set for public righteousness as for personal faith; and for public action, not negative goodness.

Faith is therefore a life practically devoted above all things to the righteousness of God, its New Creator in Christ. But in Christ means in history. A people with little or no historic consciousness cannot grasp it. It is a life of love devoted not to kindness alone but to righteousness, to righteousness concrete and not abstract, historic and not ideal nor remote. And it is devoted to a righteousness already set up and not merely indicated; and set up by a national action amid the whole context of the actual history of nations. Even Christ had not to readjust the jarred nature of God, but to secure His righteous Kingdom among men, to satisfy God's *world*-righteousness, and not His internal righteousness, which never shook. Holy Father and Holy Son were never severed. Faith is thus the life-trust and active service, public no less than private, of the world-righteousness of the Kingdom, wherein is the salvation and safety both of the soul and of society. But that gives the

Church, as the trustee of that righteousness, a very vital interest not in benevolence only but in public affairs, however indirect its action may be. There is such a thing as national faith, whose form is not creed but action. It will hardly be said that the action of God's Kingdom among men is only in those operations of love which when palliative we call philanthropy or when extensive evangelisation, and which are largely in the way of repair. It surely does not fall outside those issues of positive righteousness which are involved in the business and progress of nations, in public policy for public righteousness, and public movements for the New Humanity. Faith is the soldier's loyalty to man's absolute King, and not simply the nurse's obedience to the good Physician. We trust and follow not simply the priestly side of Christ in His sacrifice but His action in His royal person. He did not come to give an ideal of sacrifice, but He shrank from no sacrifice for the holy and righteous purpose of God. He shrank neither from making such sacrifice nor from imposing the duty of it.

CHAPTER XI

THE JUDGMENT ON THE CROSS AND IN THE FIELD

THE drift of our plea has been this. Christianity, especially on its ethical side, is regeneration. Regeneration is by a way of Justification. Justification is righteousness by Grace. Grace is the merciful act of the holy love facing defiant sin and not responsive love. Being the great Act of the *holy* love, it and its justification is the action of the absolute righteousness, of the eternal and immutable morality. And it deals with actual man at his moral centre. It is God's historic treatment of the sinful conscience, of the race as it historically is. It is the greatest moral Act of Time and Eternity, the most real and creative. The second creation is much more creative than the first because it meets not a material chaos but a moral crisis. Being so ethical and so historic it has in it, therefore, the last moral principle of history and human affairs. And its revelation and principle in the historic Cross is the focus of Christian ethic, especially on the public scale, the national scale, which the Sermon does not touch.

We take one step more. Within justification is judgment. The ethical nature of the Cross, its moral normality and finality for life, does not turn only on the moral psychology of the *justification* which founds our new life ; it is pointed in the nature of our redemption as its source—as effected in an atoning act of loving and saving *judgment.* The idea of judgment has gone out of the centre of our Christian faith, and it is taking severe judgments to bring it back.

The whole question is one of the type of religion which we cherish as Christ's. It is the question whether it be dominated at last by sympathy or by righteousness, and whether exercised in a fraternal group or in a world-Church founded on the moral triumph of a world-Atonement. There is no doubt that for the Christian public of the last half century the type has undergone a great change—a change so great as to involve a departure not only from a stiff orthodoxy but from the New Testament norm. The book is reduced from a charter to a classic. Experience and its edification have taken the place of faith, its regeneration, and its confession. With the abeyance of theological and objective religion, and the prominence of a religion subjective, facile, æsthetic, or pathetic, only not regenerative, the ethical note has fallen out of piety, and especially the junior piety; or else it has been reduced from being the very nerve and nature of our atoned salvation to being a mere sequel of it, in the way of conduct on humane or honest lines. And the result is shown in an ethic of love which has lost the supremacy of conscience in a union of hearts, and the love of righteousness in the kindness of compassion. That is to say, we have lost from our idea of reconciliation the moral note always underlying it in the New Testament as a first charge, and secured in the principles of justification and judgment interior to it there (cf. 2 Cor. v. 19 and 21). The idea and claim of the holy is not felt (just as the notion of Grace had previously faded from current conceptions of love, which was too sentimental to feel the weight or sting of sin). Christianity becomes a humanitarianism abetted by Christ, and regardless theologically of holiness, historically of nations, and ethically of public judgment. But the holy love of God in the Grace of the Cross is at once the public righteousness and the intimate kindness of the world. His kindness is dearer than His righteousness, but it is His righteousness we worship. The one we praise, the other we adore. Both are in His holy and eternal Love.

But no religion can conquer, it cannot even last, unless it openly hallow the holy name, and give practical effect in its love, amid whatever suffering, to the public righteousness of God the Saviour. It must also give it concrete effect among men in nations and not simply in crowds. The religion of love holy and incarnate must be the religion of God's intrinsic righteousness in a historic way. But this is not possible for us sinners without the moral action of justification by the Grace of the Holy. Nor is that again possible without the action and the satisfaction of love's holy judgment in the manner of our justification. For the average Christian mind love and judgment are contraries; and the action of love is to provide an escape from judgment. But that is not the

Christian revelation at all. It is fatal to it. It is immoral. It is not God's account of His love in the only place where He reveals it—in the Bible, in Christ, in the Cross. Whom He loves He chastens. The love of the Father to the soul is sure; but it was exercised in judgment, and in national judgment. This national feature in the redemption marks off Christianity very sharply from the other great religion of redemption, Buddhism—and from all its mystic dilutions. It took that national form in connection with Christ's historic work for the conscience of the world. The love of God could not, even in the case of His beloved Son, in whom He was always well pleased, be severed from the public wrath of God. Not only did it fall on Christ, but Christ also, by His manner of bearing it, became the agent and mandatory of its blessed descent on the world of peoples. All judgment of the world was committed to the Son Who endured the judgment for the world of men and nations. If Christ is the Grand Exemplar of love, it was a love which both took judgment and inflicted it. The anger of God as the anger of love is without hate. And this love we must show forth as occasion and duty call. In His name we may have to punish, but without hating. As the historic servants of Christ and His Kingdom we carry out the divine judgment; and a collective nation can become the whip of small cords dutifully to scourge the instruments of unrighteousness. The just anger of a nation is the nearest thing we know to the wrath of God. It is an ignoble thing for any Christian nation to take the rape of Belgium with superior indifference, or pious detachment.

There are notions of love and reconciliation which are amiably immoral in their public effect because they are non-historic, and therefore non-moral, in their theology, because they have no place for the exercise of judgment, private or public, in that Cross of Christ whose Reconciliation is the moral principle and living norm of the New Humanity and its history. Christian love grows not out of religious instinct but out of positive Christian faith. The quality of the one is prescribed by the other. And justifying faith, with all its implicates, is not a surrogate for righteousness, it *is* righteousness. It is the supreme form of righteousness on a world scale and at a soul's depths. It is our relation to holy love in a central, personal, creative way, and not in a mere legal, levitical, theocratic way; not in the way of precept, but of moral vitality, of fellowship with the Holy, of a community of goodness. Rectitude rises above correctitude, moral sympathy above moral compliance. The new commandment does not require but inspire. Inspiration is the mode of injunction from the holy. But the holy is in standing reaction and judgment, that often outbreaks, on the wickedness of the world, on the world's repudiation of conscience and humanity. And that judgment is not translunary, and not subliminal, but it is historic, were it but by the very place and nature of the Cross. And men are its servants and agents as they are men of faith, and as the holy life abides in them to will and to do. They are its servants and agents according to the crisis of the hour and the call of occasion. If men and nations are not agents of the judgments of God then He just ignores them; or

He uses them only in the region of the sympathetic. This is a view which leaves out His saving providence with peoples, atheises the State, and condemns us but to a cloistered ethic, a stunted conscience, and a demoralising regard for mere life, success, comfort, and happiness. All these may masque in religious guise, in types of piety which turn the bones to water, and make lymph of the blood of Christ.

The starting point in our whole Christian conception of God is His holiness, the holiness of His love. The revelation of it was historic and national. And the historic and social form of that unsparing holy love is righteousness. We are saved, men and peoples, as we enter on that righteousness; and this we do by a faith which is really a union with Him, the Faithful to death. This union is not mystic and rapt chiefly, but moral, a union not with His static person but with His dynamic work and His soul outpoured. What Christ did with humanity was not simply to maintain a spotless life in its midst, but to achieve, amid extreme judgment, and under national conditions, a universal moral conquest and a racial Redemption. He unsinned humanity in His own moral victory in a national issue; which victory was so constant, so universal, and so final that He became the Conscience of the race and its moral Providence. The process and progress of the Kingdom of God in history only unfolds this final achievement of His universal person. This ethical victory was His consecration of humanity; which was not simply a touch or a mark set on it, nor effected simply by His having 'tabernacled' with us, but by a divine life of vocation achieved in a fulness of moral power at a centre of committal to Eternal Life in the midst of Time. In escaping from Christologies merely Chalcedonian and static we moralise theology, and carry Christ into the actual life and righteousness of the race. The Incarnation was not His deep and quiet habitation of human nature, as a precious chalice might be filled with priceless wine, but an active moral conquest of history, under conditions the most extreme of antagonism from evil, and especially national evil. There is no compromise between holiness and evil. One must destroy the other. And in the moral energy of Christ in His miracle of Grace, the attempted destruction of holiness by sin was turned to the death of sin by holiness. The judgment inflicted on Christ falling on His holiness, underwent a spiritual change that makes Him, in virtue of that victory, the judge of the old world and the principle of the new. And as in His blood he obediently met the worst that evil could do in antagonism, so the society whose life He is must also do. Its history works out *in extenso* what He effected *in petto.* As He judged His judges unto holiness in the central and national crisis of the world-righteousness, so His living action in the warfare and spread of the historic Kingdom among the nations must go. Christ's moral conquest was crucial and racial; and human history now transpires in Him; Whose prolonged presence acts not only in the circles that confess Him but in the judgment on those who do not. He is the ruling providence in great affairs, and the principle for all who would master them for His Name and Kingdom. He is still the chief of the Great Powers, whenever (as now) it is an issue of world-righteousness. Man is not a mass but a mosaic of nations destined to be members of each other. Men in nations must serve the Kingdom, and not merely as individuals, groups, or Churches; for a nation has a personality of its own. Human history, the history of peoples, transpires within Redemption. It is slowly bent into the history and evolution of God's forgiveness of man by judgment which makes it a new creature. The New Humanity comes by the loving and saving judgments of God in the world. History, thus read, thus made, is the passion of Christ writ large. It is salvation by blood. It is the salvation of warring man because it is the salvation of righteousness in blood, and the establishment of holiness in judgment. Mankind's acquirement of its soul is Christ's moral and bloody victory worked into detail, His Justice made to triumph, and sin made to yield its opposite. We have indeed no more wars of religion, but still war may be made religious, a duty to God, and an agent of His Kingdom. Greater and more fertile than the martyr State is the State as judge if the Cross of Christ was more of a holy judgment than a saint's martyrdom. His destruction of evil is, in the same act, the infusion of holy life, and a new future, on the wreck of Satan's kingdom. He is crucified to the world's end, said Pascal, and to the end the Atonement is worked out in history, as it was at the first, by judgment in an issue of world-righteousness; and of this judgment the righteous man or nation is made, as the Christ in history was made, the agent and executor, to the hallowing of the New Mankind. So the very catastrophe of war is subdued and enlisted in the function and service of the blood of Christ for the Kingdom and its righteousness. The great ethic is there—for war as for all else. Unless, as I have said, He is only with the ambulance and not in the trench, acting only in the Church and not in the Cabinet, only among the worshippers and not in the warriors at all, not parting the sheep and the goats on the battle edge where a nation administers His saving justice.

The 'wickedness' of our share in a war like the present for humanity and a world-righteousness is really a huge step for the moralising of politics, and for the religionising of international relations.

God in Christ came forth in sacrifice and blood for righteousness' sake. He came to magnify His holy name in a propitiation through judgment that created the new man. To trust this eternal Act of love, and make it the principle of our life's whole carriage, is faith. If we are more than moral neophytes we are committed to resist unto blood, our own or another's, striving against world-sin in its great and deadly forms, and in a real and concrete way. We can hope for a new moral world only in this moral and faithful way. Such a world is already constituted in the blood of Christ, which is the seed of the New Creation, and the principle of the new conduct. We must carry forward His creation of such a new world at His cost (for He did not thus war merely to affect a few select souls). We are regenerated in the regeneration of the race; and it is by those principles which are not merely martyr, passive, and pious, but active, warlike and redemptive whenever the great trump calls to a world-judgment as it now does. A full Christian faith is the trust and service of holy love acting as righteousness in a historic Kingdom; that is, acting at call under public and historic conditions, and not alone under the conditions of a personal pathos of pity, sympathy, fraternity, or the like. In this moral and fundamental regeneration our own past sin, private or public, cannot be allowed to arrest the duty and service of the present hour for the new and Christian humanity in its crisis of life and death. If ever we have been seduced, in the days of our ignorance, into doing anywhere what it is now Germany's policy and principle to do in its thorough way by 'absolute war' against mankind, that is no reason why, with our eyes mercifully opened, we should not start back on the edge of the abyss and help to stop the career of those who still rush to destruction. We have outgrown our Elizabethan buccaneering, our Cromwellian 'pacifications,' our Palmerstonian dictation. In Gladstone we sloughed off our Bismarck. In the last century we have gone through a political regeneration in this respect, which is shown, above all, in our treatment of India and of South Africa. But 'the world will not believe a man repents,' far less a people. Yet if we had shirked this war we should have surrendered the claim to be a Christian nation. A Christian nation is not one that carries out the precepts of the Sermon on the Mount, which never contemplated a nation, and would make a nation impossible. For a nation is not a magnified individual, and therefore cannot be the subject of such conduct as the Sermon enjoins. For Christianity love is, of course, the supreme principle, but in public relations love takes the form of mutual respect, of law, justice, liberty, and even help—especially to the weak. It does not take the form of affectionate feeling, or more than goodwill. Love in the emotional sense is impossible toward masses of people we never see, and to vamp it up as feeling reduces religion to hypocrisy. A Christian nation is one that grows in the power of owning its place and duty in the Kingdom of God as the Cross set it up; one which honours His righteousness especially where He most revealed it, in the greatest national issue ever raised—in the saving judgment of the Cross; one which does not shrink from being the agent of His purpose and judgment in the world of nations, for the New Humanity, and in defence of right, freedom, and mercy from a people's atheist and imperial ego-mania; and one which desires and promotes for all men that fulness of life and liberty which is God's gift to all. A nation is Christian according as the State comes to be served for the sake of the world-Kingdom of God, and in concern for the weak, individuals or peoples. These have most to suffer from force, egoism, insolence, and cruelty, and the fanatic of peace would leave them to it all.[1]

[1] While writing the above, I met these words from a defender of the conscientious objectors:

'We ought to remember that it is we who have made these men conscientious objectors. It is our insistence upon the

At the present hour we can hardly think of the great war except as disaster and suffering on a scale which evokes all the pathetic and consolatory side of a religion matchless in its resources of that kind.

authority of the teaching of Jesus which has made them feel—rightly or wrongly—that in loyalty to their Master they cannot take any part in military affairs.'

On which I remark, first, that Christianity is not chiefly loyalty to a Master but life in a Redeemer, i.e. life on the principle of His Redemption, i.e. in the *Holy* Spirit. Second, I note that if we have been insisting on the supreme authority of the teaching of Jesus we cannot be surprised that our pupils turn Quakers. But as Evangelical Christians we ought not so to insist. We have been rearing our neophytes wrong. The teaching of Jesus is not the foundation of Christian ethic but is to be interpreted by that which is—namely the Redemption of the Cross as the moral crisis of the world and the creator of the new conscience in historic conditions. Our present confusion is the débâcle of the didactic or epideictic theory of Christ's work, the view that treats even the Cross as but the supreme object-lesson and most impressive display of the love of God. When the idea of holy love's saving, atoning judgment in Christ's blood has gone out of the centre of Christian ethic it takes severe judgments to bring it back.

The passage I criticise went on :

'I am not myself a conscientious objector, but I am absolutely convinced that the men who at such cost to themselves are fighting English militarism at home are, at any rate, doing as much for their country as the men who are heroically fighting Prussian militarism in the trenches of Flanders. Some day, when war is over, and we recover our lost ideals, we shall repent of our silence.' The moral perspective of values is startling.

This is equivalent to saying that the worship of conscience (and individual conscience) is doing as much for the world as the worship of righteousness (and public righteousness)—which is subjectivism of a very dangerous kind, and one for which the Spirit of the Age provides many victims. If we do not take as much pains that our conscience is true, the pains we take to be true to our conscience are wasted—as a sad amount of martyrdom is, especially in the young, whose unschooled views should lead them to be content with protest and not go on to rebellion. It is more important for the public that conscience should be sound than even that it should be free. To be true to conscience is a great thing ; it is not easy. And it gives scope for a good deal of courage of the dogged kind. But it is not so hard nor so fruitful as to get the conscience true to its pole. Some might be advised to go into dock long enough to have their compass adjusted if they are to avoid shipwreck from steering by it.

But the same religion carries us farther still. It carries us higher and deeper still. It puts us on the issue of a world-righteousness and a Kingdom of God. I do not here mean that in the reflective it stirs inquiry about the righteousness of God in permitting such a thing to be. No doubt there are many who are speculating, with Job, about the theodicy of the matter, and doing so, like him, as no mere speculators. But possibly question of that kind will come more freely when the practical exigencies of the situation have been met. And the practical urgency is not merely, How shall we win? It has more to do with a world-righteousness than that. What stirs us, braces us, and sets our face most is, How shall we, in the actual situation, secure anything like a world-righteousness, morally divine in sanction, human in compass, and humane in kind, upon earth? That is what is challenged and threatened by the self-idolatry of a Force State which owns no moral allegiance. That, and no mere victory of a nation or imperialism of a race, is now the issue. It is a world issue of righteousness, put to us in a national conflict unto blood—as Christianity was at the first. How for the future are we to secure anything like a Kingdom of God on earth? How paralyse its supreme enemy for the hour?

But once this matter of urgent righteousness is settled we shall be carried into regions of question where no few are already engaged, and also in connection with the righteousness of God. With the Kingdom of God nearer at hand we shall repent. Having in a measure secured the peace of the future the conscience will turn to the principle of the past.

And it will ask God, not with a challenge to Him, 'How could you?' but, with misgiving for man, 'Why must you?' It will not be a question of theodicy but of judgment. The victor will have suffered little less than the vanquished; and, if he has any belief in moral causation in human affairs, he will turn to ask what it was, common to both, that incurred such common chastisement. For this is not a mere earthquake due to physical causes alone. More and more the moral horror of such a war will come home to those who are not past feeling, after the energy of waging it, and the flush of victory. But there will also come a moral exaltation in the great thing done. And then will be the time to urge that our horror of the convulsion is a mere reflection and index of God's horror of the sin in the civilisation which it chastens. We shall feel that the wonder is not that such things come, but that they should be so long in coming upon a society which so successfully forgets and ignores God. When Christ in Gethsemane sank and quailed it was not simply at death and suffering; it was with the horror of His insight into the sin as God saw it, and into the judgment of God upon the crime that inflicted the Cross. If they do these things on a green tree what will be done on a dry? If they treat me so who am Israel's green tree of life what will God do to an Israel sere and dead? He foresaw the year 70. So also those who are now moved to such issues as held Christ find behind the horror of death, suffering, and cruelty, the horror of wickedness and of judgment, not upon the aggressor alone but on the whole civilisation he represents in his too too thorough way. And the people may be led, in the coming and calmer days, to see behind the horror of judgment the greater moral horror of the sin whose correction the judgment is. We may gauge our tremendous old prosperity as it always appears before Him whom it always hides. This is a grief and a wound that wrings the soul of many a non-combatant whose limbs are safe while his nights are prayer. And it forms his contribution to the general sense of the solemnity of the situation, and the general pain and care. Christ suffered more than those He cured. A pain which is less poignant may be more crushing. And the penitents of the race are not among its ineffectives. Its confessors rank with its martyrs. Its intercessors are among the great Soldiers of the Kingdom.